The Great Book of
HOLLOW-CAST FIGURES

The Great Book of
HOLLOW-CAST FIGURES

NORMAN JOPLIN

New Cavendish Books
London

Dedication

To my wife Sheila
for her support and understanding throughout
the years that it took to compile this book
and for sharing the hobby with me.

First edition published in the UK
by New Cavendish books, 1993.
This paperback edition published 1999

Copyright © New Cavendish Books, 1993

Designed by Jacky Wedgwood

Cover Design Paul Bradforth

Photography by Mark Williams
Copyright © on all photographs, except where indicated otherwise,
New Cavendish Books

Editor Narisa Chakra

Production Chris Shelley

Typeset by Dorchester Typesetting Group Ltd., Dorset
Origination by J Film Process, Singapore

Printed and bound in Barcelona, Spain by Bookprint S.L.

ISBN 1 872727 78 6

ACKNOWLEDGEMENTS
I would like to thank all who contributed information over the period
that it took to compile this reference work, with special
acknowledgements to the following, without whose help in supplying
figures for photography and information, it would not have been
possible to provide a comprehensive photographic and accurate record
of the subject:
Sarah Baddiel, Alfred and Bert Barrett, Tony Bond, Britains Petite
Limited, Delores Brown, Giles Brown, Bill Brunton, Keith Bunting, Lin
and Tony Chew, Les Clarke, Christies South Kensington, Harold
Cumpstey, Richard Driver, Ron Eccles, Helen and Martin Fahie, Ken
Farmer, Row Forbes, Derek Goldberg, Ian Gissings, Tony Harrington,
John Harris, Dr Robin Kerr, Bill Kingsman, Joe Kunzelmann, Hugo
Marsh, Roger Maryon, Stephen Naegal, Bill Nutting, Bill O'Brien, James
Opie, Don Pielin, Arnold Rolak, Andrew Rose, Ed Ruby, Brian Salter,
Stewart Saxe, Jan Scroby, John Segal, Mick Sharpe, Tim Sherwood-King,
Steve and Jo Sommers, Ian and Sue Toon, Dick Tout, Toy Soldier
Parade, Shamus Wade, Brian Wicks.

I would also like to thank Angela Haigh for typing the manuscript, her
husband David for assisting with proof reading, Jacky Wedgwood for
her superb design skills and Mark Williams for his sense of humour,
patience and professional execution of the photography.

Contents

A–Z of Manufacturers

The A–Z of Manufacturers comprises a brief history of each company, when known, and photographs of the figures with detailed captions. In the Inventory of Manufacturers' Products, at the back of the book, the figures are listed with cross-reference to the photographs.

ABEL, C D

Islington, London 1898–1914

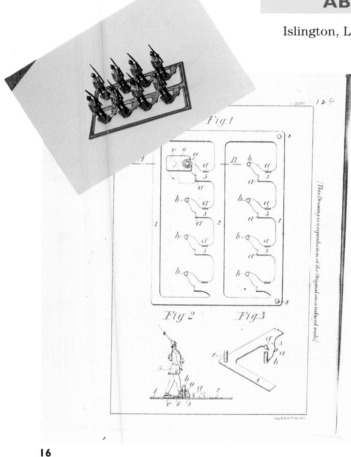

16 Original 1904 patent submission for the Abel Drill Display Frame. The photograph shows how each figure was positioned within the frame. (Photograph courtesy Bill Nutting)

17 The bases of some Abel figures had a slot to fit the Drill Display Frame, 1904.

16

17

One of the early British hollow-cast manufacturers or patenters. Formed in 1898 they ceased to operate with the outbreak of World War I. Most of their products depicted British infantry regiments, although the model of the British Camel Corps was an excellent departure from their usual fare. It is known that at least one foreign item was issued; Len Richards lists a Japanese infantry figure at the double. Abel's greatest claim to fame must be the Drill Display Frame, whereby special bases on certain foot figures enabled them to be slotted into the Drill Display Base, thus allowing the movement of up to 12 figures at once. Abel soldiers appear only to have been issued in parade positions – no action figures have so far come to light.

Bill Nutting, a US collector who has carried out much research into the early British manufacturers, suggests that Abel were patenters rather than manufacturers. It is likely that perhaps Fry, Hanks or one of the other pre-World War I manufacturers were responsible for the production of Abel figures.

ARBENZ

Birmingham, 1952

A Birmingham wholesaler to the toy trade, Arbenz and Company are thought to have purchased from Hill, Flyde and others, re-packaged and issued figures under the brand names of Azco Cards, Sovereign, Bryta, Metasol and Monarch. This complicated history is detailed within the section devoted to John Hill and Company.

18

Advertisement from *Games and Toys*, 1952, showing a selection of the Monarch range as distributed by Arbenz Ltd. The piper is a Fylde product, the Field Marshal by Hill.

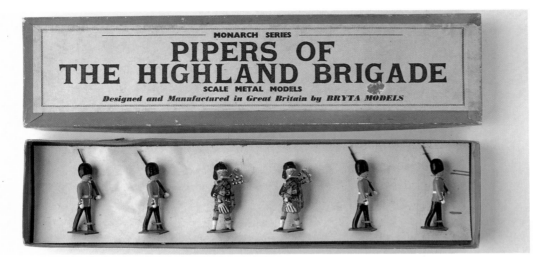

19

This 1952 boxed set causes confusion in two respects: firstly only two pipers are included and secondly, although they are contained in a 'Monarch' box issued by Arbenz, the manufacture is attributed to Bryta and the contents are clearly by John Hill (guards) and Fylde Manufacturing Company (pipers).

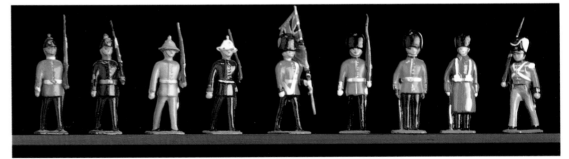

20

20 The first six figures were issued under the 'Monarch' trade name: infantry of the line, Royal Army service corps, Malta Regiment, Royal Marines, guards standard bearer and guardsman at the slope. The next two figures were found in boxes marked 'Metasol' and the Waterloo Grenadier came in a 'Sovereign' Series Azco card box. All were probably made by John Hill in 1952.

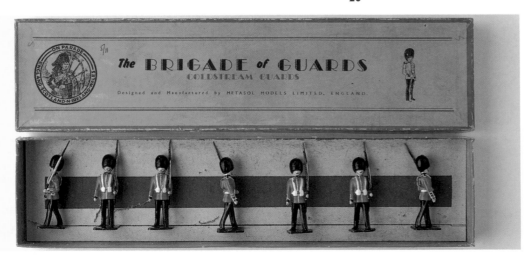

21 This box contains John Hill figures dated 1952, here packed in a 'Metasol' box. (They are also found in 'Monarch' boxes.)

21

22

Argosy die-cast figures of Peter the Dog, Peregrin the Penguin, Louise the Lamb and Muffin the Mule, 1953.

ARGOSY

London, 1953

Argosy are known to have produced die-cast figures of Muffin the Mule and some of his friends.

ASTRA

London, 1935–1960

Astra Pharos commenced production of a range of die-cast army guns and accessories in 1935 and continued after the war extending their ranges and introducing traffic signals and harbours with working lights. Astra was bought out by John Hill and Company during the late 1950s by which time Hill were fast approaching bankruptcy. It is therefore uncertain if John Hill actually marketed Astra products before going out of business in early 1960.

A V H FARM TOYS

London, 1954

A V H, Olson and Kayron were probably wholesale agents. The boxed sets that were issued during the 1950s included die-cast horses pulling a series of tinplate and wire farm implements. All were out of scale, being larger than the standard 54mm scale figures produced by hollow-cast manufacturers of the day. An example of the tin and wire horse-drawn farm implement is illustrated in the section devoted to unidentified figures.

BARRETT & SONS

See Taylor & Barrett, pages 217-238

23

Example of original box and gun manufactured in 1947 by Astra prior to their take-over by John Hill.

23A

George Bernard Shaw (a close friend of WJ Bassett-Lowke) in discussion with Lloyd George. A series of six personality figures were available between 1925 and 1939. They were all in fact solid castings and excellent reproductions have been made in recent times.
(See also pages 61 and 309)

BASSETT-LOWKE LTD

Northampton, 1899 – present day

Commissioned William Britain to produce a series of railway personality passengers to fit with 'O' gauge trains. George Bernard Shaw, Charlie Chaplin, Amy Johnson, Ramsey McDonald, Lloyd George and Groucho Marx were produced and issued in individual boxes.

BMC

Brighton and London, 1916–1933

Britannia Model Company changed its brand name to Soldarma after clashing with John Hill and Company, who had already registered Britannia Brand as a trade name. B M C, as they are usually referred to, produced an extensive range of military figures both in action and in parade drill between 1916 and 1933. The figures, although of very good design and quality, lacked consistency when it came to scale and were often 60mm or 45mm as opposed to the standard 54mm. The originality of castings, in particular cavalry items, helped to establish B M C as one of the country's main 'early' competitors to Britains. Several non-military items were produced and must be considered some of the earliest and rarest. James Opie puts forward the theory that perhaps the initials 'B M C' stand for Brighton Model Company. This follows the discovery of a descriptive price list showing Waterline Ship models, a line known to have been produced by B M C.

A selection of figures produced c.1920
Top row: mounted French, Scots Grey and Russian officers.
2nd row: rare khaki World War I bicycle troop, very rare senior naval officer, three sizes of Household Cavalry.
3rd row: three Indian chiefs carrying different weapons, crawling Indian and cowboy with revolver.
(Courtesy James Opie)

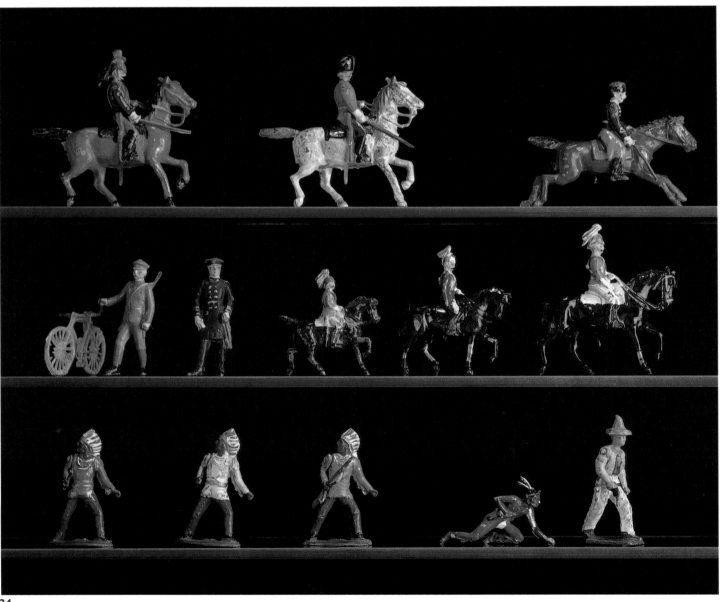

24

25 Boxes for 60mm BMC figures, c.1920.
(Courtesy James Opie)

26 Boxes for 54mm BMC figures, c.1920.
(Courtesy James Opie)

27 Cowboy and Indian boxes, c.1920. The box containing the cowboys is an incomplete set.
(Courtesy Helen and Martin Fahie)

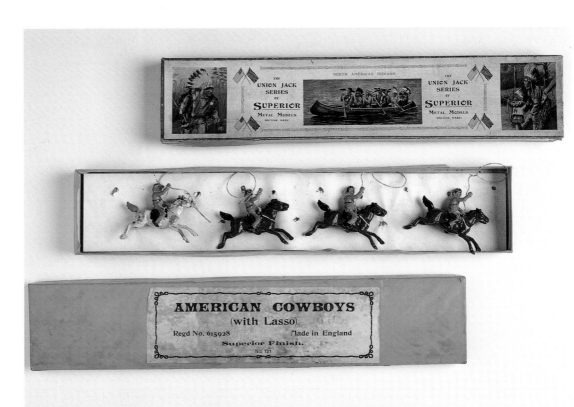

3rd row: country clergyman (593), shepherd with lamb (594), shepherd boy with lantern (595), mounted gentleman farmer (598), boy on Shetland pony (600), Guide mistress (607), traffic policeman (621), huntswoman mounted astride (623), policeman peak cap (659), navvy with pickaxe (645), navvy with shovel (646), milk roundsman (652).

All available pre- and post-war except for numbers 531, 554, 557, 558, 561, 562, 578, 587, 592 and 607 which were pre-war only. (Courtesy Ian and Sue Toon)

48

Farm animals
Top row: shire-horse (506), shire colt (507), cow (508), calf (509), sheep walking (510), sheep feeding (511), lamb (512), dog (513), pig (514), turkey (515), speckled fowl (516), white fowl (517), angry gander (519).
2nd row: goose (520), sheep lying (521), duck (533), calf lying (534), sheep lying with lamb (536), cow lying (538), cow feeding (539), goat (540), cart horse (541), horse feeding (543), chicks, pecking, standing and running (544).

3rd row: sitting hen (545), piglets feeding and walking (546), cob (550), donkey (552), goslings (565), dog lying (571), dog sitting (572), bull (573), St Bernard dog (576), Berkshire pigs, boar and sow (596).
All were available pre- and post-war except number 517, which was pre-war only.
(Courtesy Ian and Sue Toon)

49

Farm animals
Top row: 'Exmoor Horn' ram and ewe (597), Jersey cow (599), Hampshire Down ram (601), foal (602), rabbit (603), cat (604).
2nd row: greyhound standing (605), greyhound running (606), hare (620), swan and cygnets (622), rabbit sitting up (636), begging dog (637), spiteful cat (638), white leghorn hen (643). Highland cattle (647).
3rd row: field horses (648-649), bull, tail down (573) (post-war).
All available pre- and post-war except 636–38 (pre-war only). 573 is a post-war version of a pre-war item.

3rd row: young rhinoceros (960), lion cub (962), gazelle (963), sea lion
(964), Himalayan bear (965), polar bear walking (966), polar bear standing
(967), Indian or water buffalo (968), giant panda (969), baby pandas (970).
(Courtesy Ian and Sue Toon)

64

A cardboard Noah's Ark (1550) issued in 1939 with Eastern people to represent Noah and his family, together with various pairs of animals from the Zoo Series.

Eastern people issued in boxed sets (1313, 1314) pre- and post-war including palm trees, camel, goat and donkey. See also **64**.
(Photograph courtesy *Toy Soldier Parade*)

65

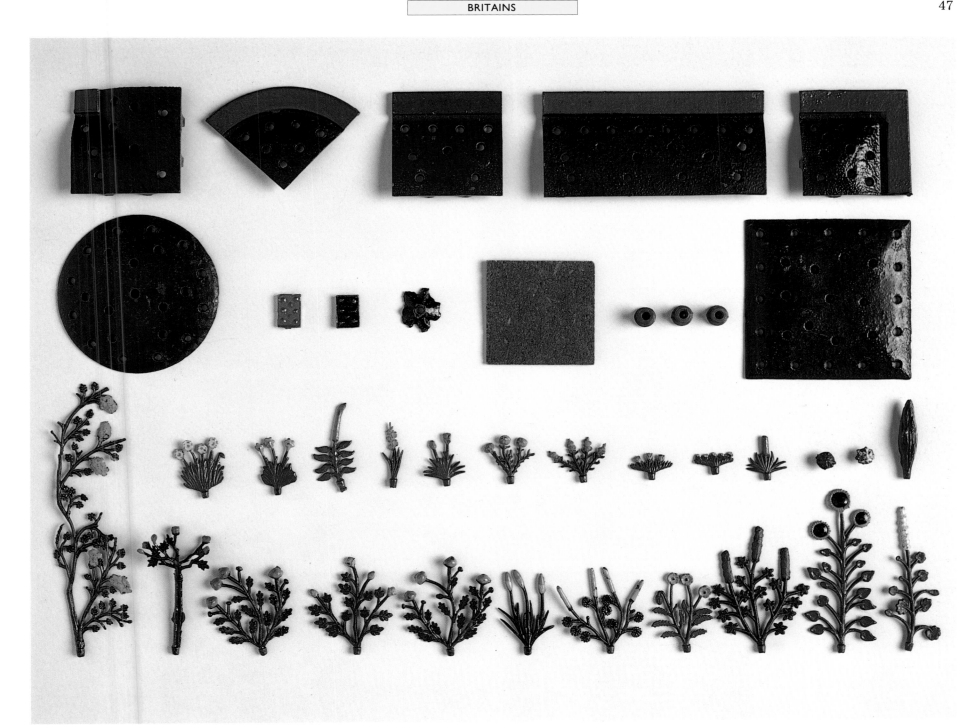

66

Pre-war garden items
Top row: flower beds; return square section (03), finishing circular section (02), half straight section (05), straight section (01), finishing corner section (06).
2nd row: round bed (065), seed boxes (069), earth mound (015), cork lawn (049), flower pots (059) and square bed (066).
3rd row: rambler rose (019) (and below), daffodil (044), aster (029), foxglove (036), gladioli (034), tulip (041), geranium (021), antirrhinum (031), crocus (042), snowdrop (043), hyacinth (040), lobelia (020), sweet alyssum (046), conifer (023).
4th row: half standard rose (027), dahlia (double) (032), dahlia (single) (033), chrysanthemum (037), torch lily (022), lupin (026), poppy (025), delphinium (039), sunflower (024), hollyhock (030).
(Courtesy Ian and Sue Toon)

Pre-war garden flower beds
displaying the variety of
permutations that can be achieved
with the range of Britains flowers.
(Courtesy Ian and Sue Toon)

67

Pre-war garden items
Interlaced board fence with trellis
(018), rustic arch (014), flint wall
square corner section (629), straight
section (624), short cross section
(628), gate posts and gate (633, 634
and 630), stile (626), stone wall
(012), sundial (010), wooden blocks
for varying levels of terracing (060),
step ladders (31), cold frame (064),
man pushing lawnmower (051),
balustrading (061), balustrading
short section (062), lawn section
(049), upper and lower rockery
steps (057 and 058), rockery outer
corner (056), rockery straight (054),
rockery inner return corner (055),
crazy paving (09), square tub (047),
round tub (016), post for
balustrading (063) and post for
stone walling (07).
(Courtesy Ian and Sue Toon)

68

Pre-war greenhouse (053), garden
shelter (28mg) and fully modelled
tree (31mg) which has a central
spiked trunk enabling the branch
sections to be slotted in.
(Courtesy John Harris)

69

108

110

108 Very rare Edwardian family, 1908; mother and father seated, baby, daughter and son.

109 Souvenir items made in 1935 for Madame Tussauds Waxworks: Madame Tussaud bust, Cinderella seated on barrel, Little Red Riding Hood, King Henry VIII, Queen Elizabeth I.

110 Lloyd George, one of the personality figures produced by Britains in 1937 for Bassett-Lowke.

111 Post-war greyhound with special 'Made in England' tag attached to comply with United States import requirements. (Courtesy Tim Sherwood-King)

111

109

112

Canadian Pacific Railway engine paperweight issued during the 1924 British Empire Exhibition at Wembley. (Photograph courtesy *Toy Soldier Parade*)

Examples of the large range of solid items made by Carman during the 1930s. Most periods of military costume were manufactured with a particular emphasis on personality figures; the bottom row shows King Henry VIII with one of his wives, George III, Hamlet, Wellington, Bonnie Prince Charlie and Nelson. The action figure in the row above depicts Rob Roy.

CARMAN

London, 1930

Carman figures, although solid, were popular with collectors during the 1930s. A wide range of historical figures were produced depicting the uniforms of the British army, emphasis being placed on the Napoleonic period. A number of personality figures were included within the substantial range. Mr Carman was one of the founder members of the British Model Soldier Society and his products still find favour with its members.

114 Cartwright footballer manufactured in 1909 for inclusion in boxed sets sold through Lord Kitchener's Workshop. The pin in the footballer's head operates the kicking leg.

115 Post-war cow, racehorse and jockey found in the racing game 'Escalado' by Chad Valley.

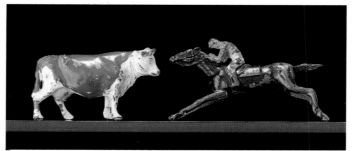

115

116 One of a series of cardboard soldiers on wooden blocks issued by Chad Valley in 1937.
(Courtesy Helen and Martin Fahie)

117 Chad Valley cardboard fort with working drawbridge, 1910. The whole piece is designed to fold flat into the box used as the base for the fort. The gilt soldiers were probably by Hanks.
(Courtesy James Opie)

114

CARTWRIGHT

Rotherhithe, London, 1923

Known to have made a footballer with a pin in his head which moved a kicking leg. Cartwright operated from Prospect Street, Rotherhithe and first advertised a range of 'Cheap' and 'Good Quality' toy soldiers in *Games and Toys* in 1923.

The football figures were supplied to Lord Kitchener's Workshop for ex-servicemen to thread, card and package. Positive identification of the rest of the Cartwright range has not been possible. However, some of the items pictured in the section devoted to unidentified figures may be Cartwright products.

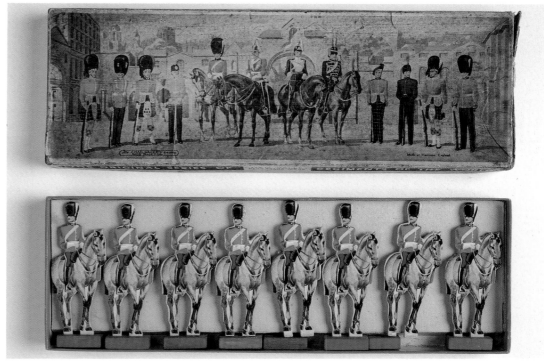

116

CHAD VALLEY

Birmingham, 1920–1972

Chad Valley, one of the best known firms amongst British toy manufacturers, rarely ventured into lead figures. It is possible that other companies were responsible for the production of lead figures for inclusion in various games produced by Chad Valley. 'Escalado', a race game made in the early 1920s, came supplied with lead horses and jockeys and a cardboard fort, was supplied with gilt painted soldiers probably manufactured by Reka. Cardboard soldiers on wooden bases came packed in most attractive illustrated boxes and were issued in 1937.

117

CHARBENS

Hornsey, London, 1920–1966

The firm was founded by Charles and Benjamin Reid in the early part of the 1920s, the name being derived from a combination of the brothers' first names. One of the brothers was a former employee of William Britain and it is assumed that hollow- and die-casting techniques were learnt during this period. The brothers subcontracted to Taylor & Barrett before the latter issued their own ranges. The first advertisements for the company appeared in the toy trade journal *Games and Toys* in December 1927, when a series of farmyard novelties are mentioned. The company's production prior to World War II consisted predominantly of non-military items, in which most of the figures and accessories were hollow-cast, while vehicles etc. were die-cast. Post-war production was equally split between military and non-military products. However, very few of the pre-war lines were reissued after the war, the exceptions being the circus range.

The firm operated from Hornsey Road in North London up until the mid-1960s when lead production was phased out in favour of plastic. Lead items by Charbens were distributed via wholesale outlets to toy shops. Distribution was patchy, and Len Richards commented in a mid-1950s article in the British Model Soldier Society's *Bulletin* 'that only one Toy Shop in twenty stocked Charbens products'.

Charbens, although producing their own unique ranges of figures, did have connections with other makers. A pre-war catalogue, believed to be dated 1932, shows several items that are known to have been available from other manufacturers, among them the Miniature Hunt, (see John Hill and Company). This series of miniature solid items could have been produced on the continent and sold in the UK through Charbens and Hill. Circus items and dolls' house furniture were also packaged and sold via the firm of Kay, who specialised in packaging other companies' products under their own name (see page 172). Post-war connections were with Saalheimer and Company, a toy importer, wholesaler and distributor, who issued Charbens vehicles and accessories under the trade name 'Salco', together with a variety of die-cast Disney characters. It is uncertain, but likely, that the Disney items were also made by Charbens. (See also Salco). Charbens also used W Fasham and Sons and E A Thorne as agents for their products, discounting the theory suggested by previous authors that these agents were manufacturers.

The identification of Charbens items is usually quite easy, although not all items are marked. 'RD' was used pre-World War II. This trade mark could have denoted 'registered design', or perhaps it was taken from the first and last letters of the founders' surname. The name Charbens appeared on some of the pre-war horse-drawn vehicles, but in most cases only post-war items carried the Charbens name. 'C and Co' has been found on some items but these are few and far between. A number of horse-drawn items marked 'Mimic' were issued pre-war. Post-World War II 'Cecil Series' was used on some sets.

Farm Series
Illustrated pre-war reference material on Charbens Farm Series has not been discovered.

Pre-war issues:
Top row: feeding cockerel, dog and trotting Shetland pony.
2nd row: gamekeeper with shotgun, gun dog carrying fowl and seated fixed arm farmer's wife.

Post-war issues:
Top row: shire-horse, goat with bell and bull.
2nd row: wheatsheaf, milkmaid walking, milkmaid milking and farmer with walking stick with gold watch chain on waistcoat.

119

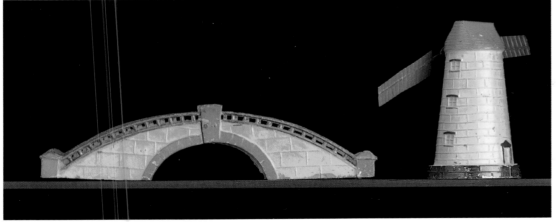

120

119 Circus figures

Available pre- and post-war as either single items or in boxed display sets of varying sizes. Details of pre-war issues can be found in the relevant section of the inventory.

Clown on stilts described by Charbens as 'Longman'; juggler; elephant balancing on tub; parrot on perch with feeding bowls; trapeze artists on wire; clown climbing ladder with bucket of water; 'Fairy' (equestrienne) on horseback; clown holding hoop and performing dog; clown riding unicycle; laughing clown with hands in pockets; acrobat balancing on chair; elephant with outstretched trunk; acrobat riding cycle; clown policeman; seal balancing ball on nose; ringmaster with wire whip; strongman with barbells; boxing midgets; very rare circus girl in drum majorette uniform with arms raised; liberty horses. Each item in this most imaginative series could be obtained in various paint styles.

120 Rare pre-war bridge and windmill. The windmill has tinplate sails.

Top row: motor cycle policeman; policeman on point duty, also issued in the Road Works display set; rare postman; bus stop; police motor cycle and sidecar combination and telephone box with opening door.
2nd row: soap box racer being pushed by Cub Scout with Cub Scout passenger; Cub Scout throwing stone, all three Cubs also came dressed in blue; seated flower seller with basket; goat cart with girl passenger, a red cart with girl in red dress and pulled by a white harnessed goat was also available.
3rd row: items from the Hikers' Set which also contained a lead tent marked the 'Hikery', a rug and various cups, saucers, plates etc. Female hiker with backpack and stick, male hiker resting, seated female hiker reading a book and male hiker with backpack and stick.
4th row: Boy Scout kneeling with pole, patrol leader with pole, two Scouts with movable arms carrying axe and bugle. All four Scouts are considered very rare.
With the exception of the telephone box, all items in this illustration were issued pre-war only.

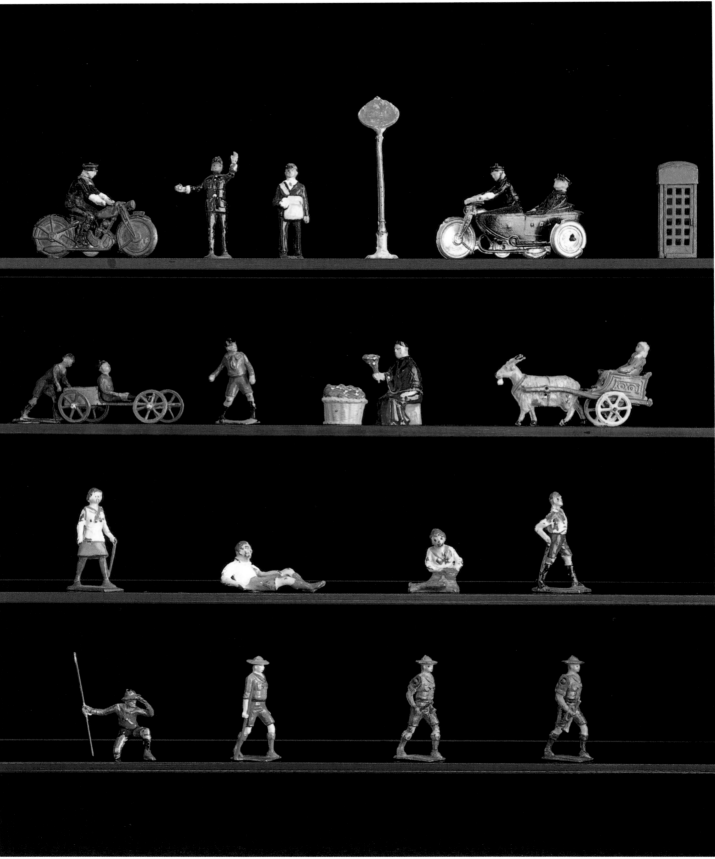

143

Post-war military figures

The United States Army GI figures illustrated in rows one and two are very similar to the Timpo series with the notable exception of the wounded soldier on crutches pictured top row, fifth from the left.
Top row: standard bearer with stars and stripes, marching slung rifle, kneeling radio operator with aerial and orders, motorcycle and rider, wounded on crutches, head bandaged, wounded arm in sling, stretcher party.
2nd row: charging fixed bayonet, mine detector and operator, grenade thrower with rifle, advancing with automatic weapon, mortar and operator, kneeling field wireless operator, crawling with rifle, lying firing rifle, kneeling firing rifle, seated machine gunner.

3rd row: British infantry stabbing with bayonet, charging, clubbing with rifle; seated machine gunner, whose gun has a spring loading device and a pin which slots into the machine gunner's hand enabling matchsticks to be fired when released; green beret patrol leader, a scarce version of the red beret pictured to his right; red berets with flame thrower, standing firing foot on rock, kneeling firing and grenade thrower; khaki Highlander at slope, fixed arm.

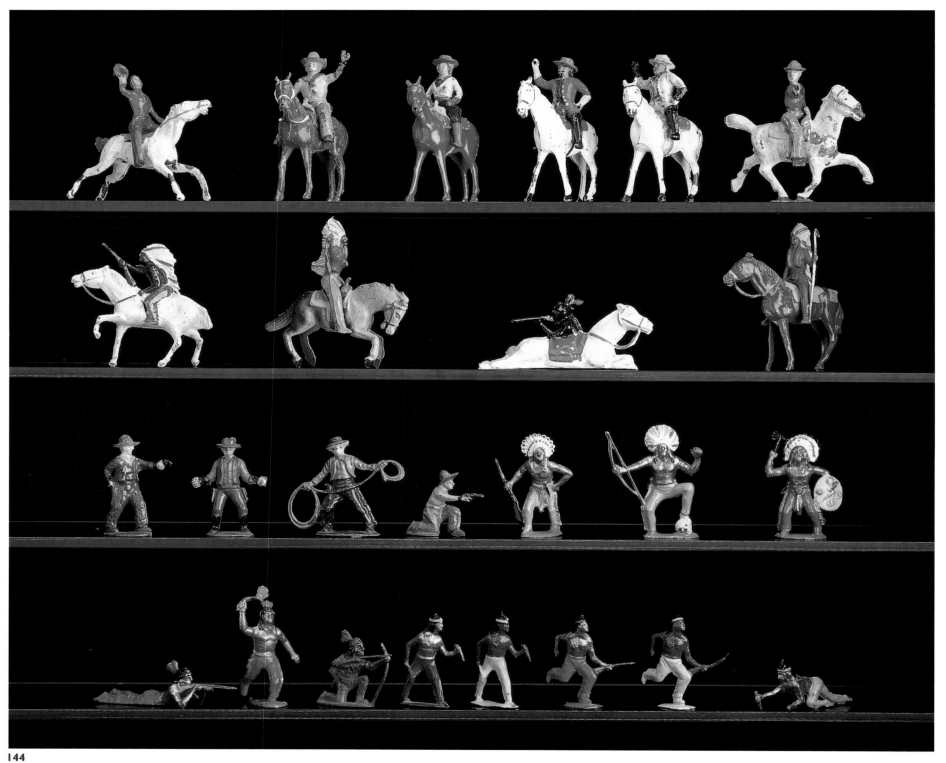

144

Top row: pre-war cowboy mounted waving hat in air, detachable from the horse, as are the following post-war items in this row; cowboy to hold lasso, cowgirl, Royal Canadian Mounted Police, Buffalo Bill, cowboy firing pistol on trotting horse.
2nd row: Indian chief mounted with rifle; Indian chief mounted with rifle, detachable from horse; Indian brave sitting firing rifle from behind lying horse, probably subcontracted from John Hill; chief on standing horse with movable arm. All pre-war.

3rd row: cowboy firing pistol, gunslinger, cowboy with lasso, cowboy kneeling firing, Indian chief with rifle, Indian chief with bow and arrow with foot resting on scull, Indian chief with shield and tomahawk. Post-war.
4th row: braves lying firing rifle, running with flaming torch, kneeling firing bow and arrow, two paint variations of brave with knife, two variations running with rifle, crawling with knife. Post-war.

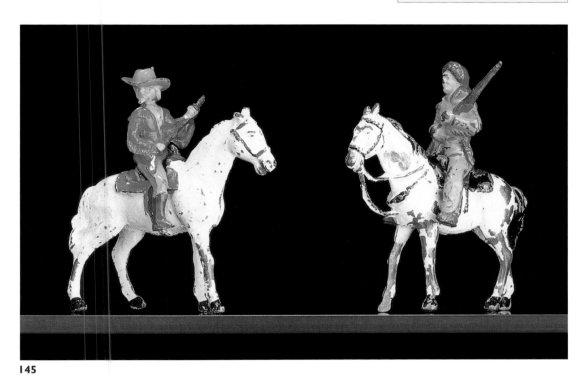

145

146

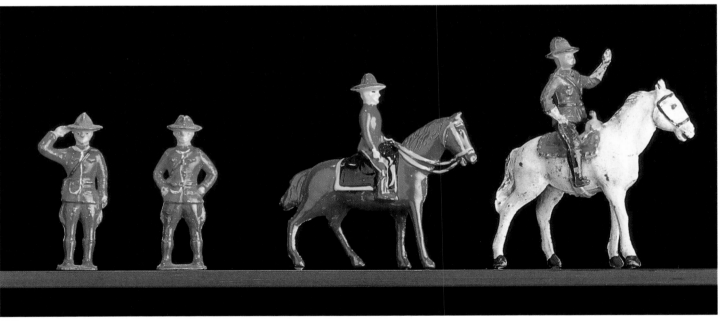

147

145 Two rare western personality figures of Buffalo Bill and Davy Crocket, 1954.
(Photograph courtesy Brian Wicks)

146 This very rare Robin Hood figure is similar to the Crescent Robin Hood, but is a modern reproduction made and kindly given to me by Mrs Jan Scroby of Marlborough Military Models, who recently acquired the Charbens moulds.

147 Post-war Royal Canadian Mounted Police. Three 50mm examples saluting, with hands on hips and mounted. The fourth larger figure is removable from his horse.

Medieval figures, 1953. Supplied in a silver-plated type finish: attacking with sword, mounted knight on armoured horse, knight with sword and shield, knight standing with sword and shield. Feathers of different colours were sometimes added to these figures giving the headress a plumed appearance.

148

Spacemen. Probably the last hollow-cast figures to be issued by Charbens around 1958, designed by Wilfred Cherrington. The shortlived production accounts for their rarity. Perspex helmets similar to the Cherilea and Hill space figures were used and it is possible that more figures exist in this range.

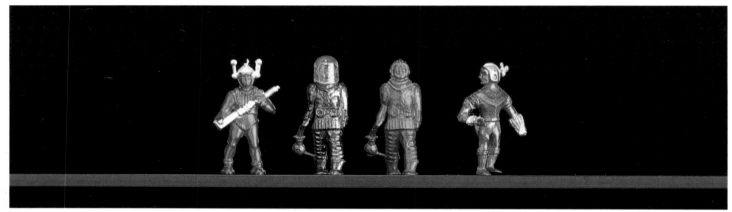

149

Drum majorettes boxed set, 1954. Probably the rarest of all Charbens sets, made only for the United States and sold under the Andover Series label. Contains five majorettes with raised hands based on the pre-war circus girl, an adaptation of the figure with a baton and a cheerleader with megaphone. (I am indebted to Bill O'Brien of Princetown, New Jersey USA for the discovery and acquisition of this set.)

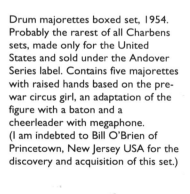

150

CRESCENT TOY COMPANY

London, 1922

The Crescent Toy Company was founded in 1922. It was not until 1932 that Crescent took the opportunity to establish themselves as lead figure manufacturers, when they bought the moulds and stock of C W Baker, who had traded as Reka (see Reka). Charles G Rason was a leading light in the company which was situated at 6–8 Fountayne Road, London N15.

The majority of figures issued prior to World War II were reissues of the Reka range, although not all Reka figures were thought worthy of production. Crescent issued a wartime catalogue which illustrated part of the former Reka range, together with additional items which may have been purchased from the redundant stocks of other manufacturers. As there was no consistent pattern of figure production before World War II, it is difficult to ascertain which figures were actually manufactured by Crescent.

The subject area of Crescent's figures was mainly military, with the occasional farm item included; a policy which was to change after World War II. In common with other manufacturers the pre-war cataloguing system was somewhat confusing. This policy was changed during the post-war period.

A 1949 edition of *British Playthings* gives a potted history of Crescent, listing the owners as Mr A Schneider, Mr H Eagles and Mr A Eagles. The article boasts that Crescent toys were exported world-wide with a large number going to America. As well as hollow-cast figures a certain amount of die-cast items were produced. The content of production swung from military to items of a non-military nature as war-like toys took a dive in popularity after World War II. Crescent had connections with other companies during the late 1940s, one of which was D C M T (Die-Cast Metal Tools) for whom Crescent issued die-cast vehicles. This connection is relevant when mentioning two of the partners in Crescent, Messrs A and H Eagles. Upon the death of Mr A Eagles, Harvey Eagles left Crescent to start the toy company of Harvey, producing his own range of hollow-cast figures (see Harvey). Harvey Eagles later sold his trade name 'Harvey Series' to D C M T who issued plastic figures using the trade name Lone Star. During the 1950s, Crescent opened a large factory in Cwmcarn in Monmouthshire to cope with the increased production of their successful ranges of hollow-cast figures. By 1960, hollow-cast items were phased out in favour of plastic.

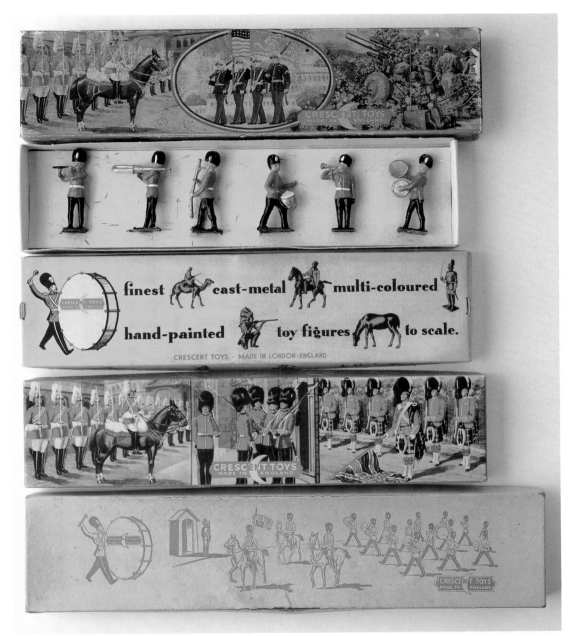

170

Four versions of 1950s boxes which contained the common post-war Guards bandsmen.
(Courtesy Helen and Martin Fahie)

171

Top row: guardsmen: officer saluting, two versions standing firing, at ease, on guard, at slope, kneeling firing, presenting arms, marching with movable slope arm. Only two movable arm figures were issued by Crescent, the other being a West Point Cadet. All post-war.
2nd row: guardsman in greatcoat with sentry box, second version Guards bandsmen with fife, cymbals, tuba, trombone and bugle, coronation official, state trumpeter and tinplate sentry box. All post-war.
3rd row: rare pre-war Guards drum major. The following nine Guards

bandsmen were also issued by Reka: fife, trombone, tuba, side drum, cymbals, bugle and three versions of bassoon. The last figure in this row is a scarce figure of a bass drummer, minus drum. All post-war
4th row: kneeling firing Highlander in feather bonnet, Highlanders in pith helmets kneeling at the ready, two lying firing with legs together and legs apart, kneeling, lying and marching at the slope. Highlanders in 50mm scale: piper, die-cast guardsmen at attention, standard bearer, saluting and Life Guard. All post-war.

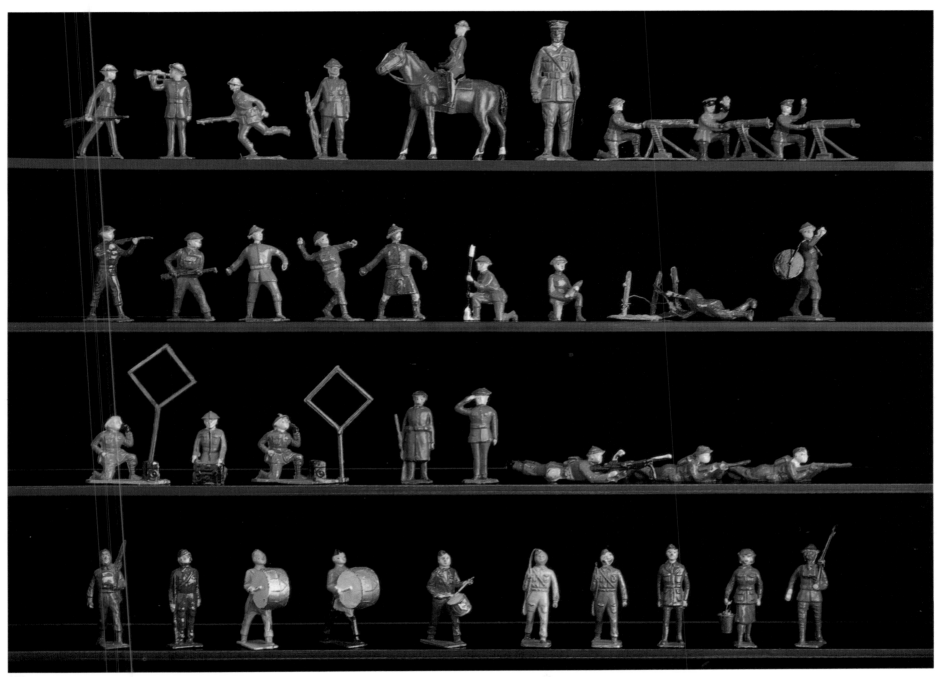

172

Top row: apart from the mounted figure, all were issued between 1932 – 1939. Steel helmet marching at the trail; bugler (reissued in green helmet or sand-coloured uniform, 1950s); running trail; at ease; mounted officer, detachable from horse, used for Life Guard etc. (post-war); 70mm officer in World War I uniform (probably inherited by Crescent from a rival manufacturer); steel helmet machine gunner; two paint variations of peak cap machine gunner with raised arm. Khaki was sometimes repainted with red or blue when khaki uniforms fell from favour.
2nd row: all issued pre- and post-war. Standing firing rifle; advancing fixed bayonet; grenade thrower (this and the Scottish version fifth left were former 'Fry' items); raised arm grenade thrower, reissued in the 1950s with green helmet and sand coloured ranges; kneeling with mobile rocket launcher; kneeling with shell; barbed wire entanglement and man with

wire cutters; Royal Signals with role of wire from set no. NN700.
3rd row: the first three items are from set no K703 Field Wireless Unit. The diamond shape wireless aerial on figure one is the second version mounted on top of the wireless; the first version with the aerial secured by a ring to the side of the wireless is item 3; item 2 is kneeling with generator and head phones. A pre-war figure at ease in greatcoat is followed by four post-war items: peak cap officer saluting, large scale lying baren gunner, two lying firing rifles the second with forage cap.
4th row: slope arms, Home Guard, bass drummers, side drummer, two with slung rifles, officer walking, a paint variation of the RAF officer, two rare figures of Women's Auxiliary Territorial Service, and a slope arm figure adapted to wear a gas mask (held in place over the face by inserting a pin through the chest). All post-war.

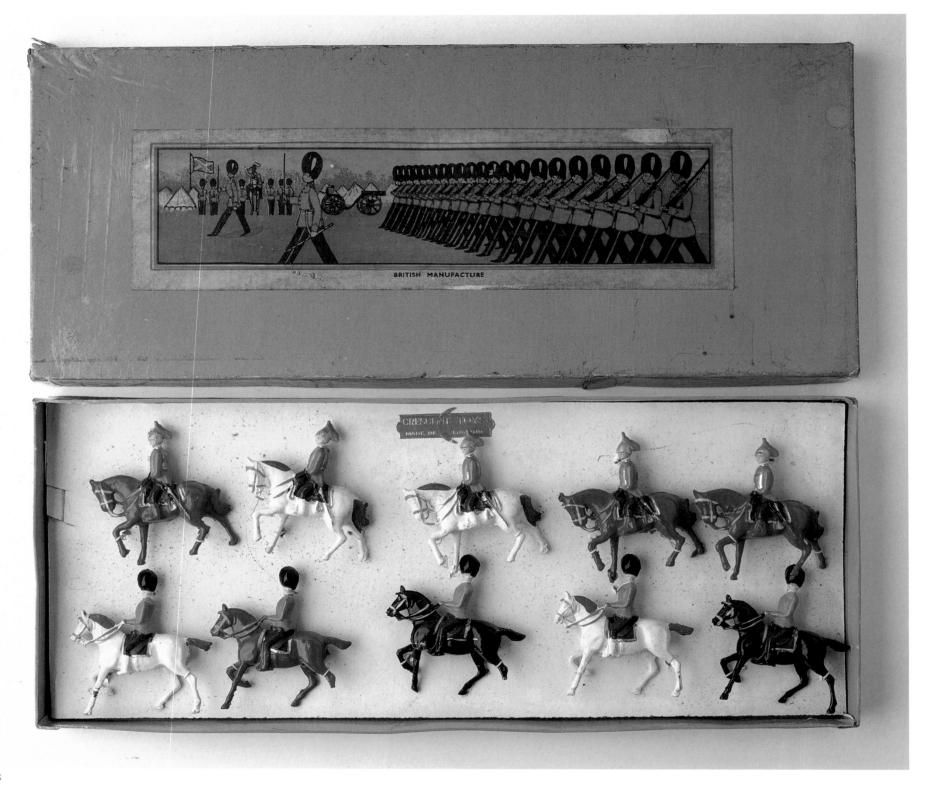

173

Boxed set issued pre-war containing mounted Life Guards and guardsmen.

174

Top row: Arab with rifle on camel, (pre- and post-war), Sikh standing easy, Indian Army lancer, Sikh officer at attention, European riding elephant. The three Indian figures were produced pre-war only.
2nd row: post-war Royal Canadian Mounted Police: firing pistol, at ease, kneeling, mounted officer turned in saddle, kneeling firing, firing rifle, at slope.
3rd row: Arab with Scimitar, seated Arab (two paint versions), African

tribesman with rifle, Maori warrior adapted from the former Reka Zulu figure, North African infantry, French Foreign Legion at slope, North African bugler (paint variation of the Guards bugler), a rare French Foreign Legion standard bearer. All post-war.
4th row: movable and fixed arm West Point cadets at slope, foot and mounted highwaymen, pirate with pistol, German officer in greatcoat, Zulu (another former Reka product). All pre-war except item one.

Medical figures

Top row: four paint versions of stretcher party. Post-war in sand-coloured uniform and three pre-war versions, of which the first two represent St John's Ambulance and civilian services, the third is the common khaki example.

2nd row: three wounded men, kneeling military and civilian nurses and a 40mm walking nurse of pre-war vintage.

175

176 Pre-war catalogue page showing gun teams which were former Reka products.

177 Catalogue page from 1939 showing ships, utensils and khaki gun team produced prior to 1932 by Reka.

176

177

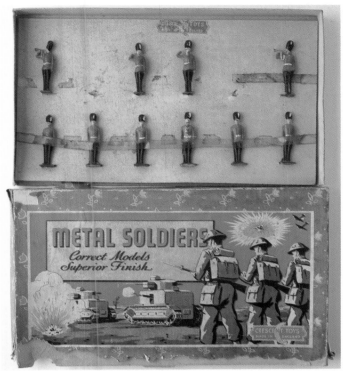

178

A rare boxed set (incomplete) containing die-cast utility soldiers made during the early post-war period.

179

Colourful box lids for Crescent toys were a feature of the company's marketing strategy in the 1950s. A tinplate sectional fort is contained in the box at the top, the 'Whitehall' box held a tinplate sentry box with mounted Life Guard, while the box at right contained a US mortar set. (Courtesy James Opie)

201

203

204 Garden tea party and box, 1950. This rare boxed item consists of table with umbrella, four chairs, two boys, two girls and various cups, saucers and plates.

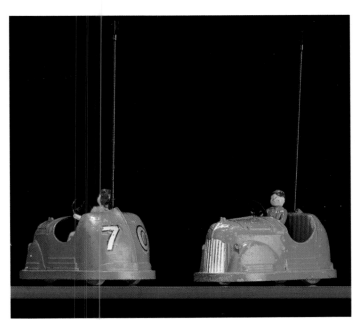

202

201 Grandad and Grandma set with original box, 1954. Seated grandad with stick, grandma with knitting, bench seat, table, cups and plates and pet dog.

202 Two very rare dodgem cars, 1952. Each has a flint which sparks as the cars are moved. The same children are used in the milk bar, children's hospital, tea party, School Days set and Junior Miss set.

203 Junior Miss dressing table, comb, hairbrush and makeup, with seated Miss, 1950.

204

School days, 1950. Male teacher at desk, female dunce, boy and girl seated at desks, female teacher, blackboard and easel, male dunce and school crossing or 'lollipop' man (the cardboard sign from the 'lollipop' pole is missing).

206 Children's hospital with sister, nurse and doctor, 1950. Beds with linen bedclothes, boy patients in blue pyjamas, girl in pink and baby in shawl. The original boxed set had flower vases and bowls of fruit to stand on the bedside cabinets. All are die-cast and prone to lead fatigue.

207 Children's hospital poem.

205

206

CRESCENT TOYS
MADE IN ENGLAND

THE CHILDREN'S HOSPITAL

"IN THE WARD"
(By a Hospital Matron.)

When I had a pain the Doctor said
I must go to Hospital — stay in bed
So here I am in a dear little ward
With Daphne, Anne and baby Maud.

Every morning at five to eight
The day nurses come in — they're never late
They bath us all and then brush our hair
I clean my teeth with greatest care.

Breakfast to eat and beds to be made
Ten o'clock comes, time that baby is weighed
She has a bottle, Daphne has malt
I have medicine that tastes like salt.

When Doctor comes he says I am good
I've taken my medicine just as I should
He looks at my tongue and feels my pain
Now it's better — won't come again.

Sister gives me a lovely dinner
'Cos she wants me fatter not thinner·
There's time for a sleep and time for tea
Time for play for Daphne and me.

There's a motor car with seat at back
There's even Childrens' hour and Uncle Mac
Then time for supper and time for bed
Hands to be washed — prayers to be said.

Night nurse is coming — she'll keep one small light
And not put it out although it is night
She'll stay till morning — not go away
I'll be a nurse like that, one day.

207

208 'Our Doggies' set and original box, 1950. Cardboard backdrop, kennel, dog standing, dog feeding from bowl and 'Beware of the Dog' sign. Bones and biscuits in lead were also issued in this set.

209 Leaflet from the 'Our Doggies' set encouraging children to join the 'Tail Waggers Club'.
(Courtesy Helen and Martin Fahie)

210 A page from Hobday Brothers catalogue, 1951, illustrating a number of the non-military sets available at the time.

208

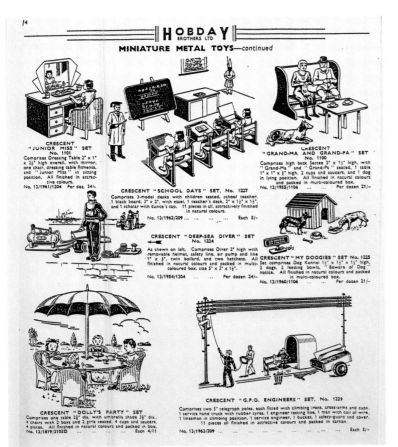

210

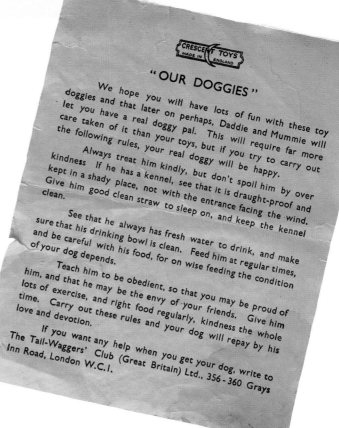

209

GPO Telephone Engineers' set, 1950. Die-cast barrow with rubber tyres, telegraph poles, engineer with coil of wire, engineer climbing telegraph pole, engineer kneeling with headphones. Tinplate hut and accessories. A mixture of hollow-cast, die-cast and tinplate make up this set.

211

Tuglift and Builder's and Decorator's Truck, 1951. The tuglift box illustrates the item which is always found in a fatigued state. The builder's and decorator's truck contains bucket, ladder, saw, whitewash brush and various other die-cast tools.

212

213

214

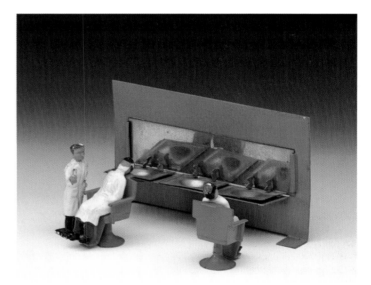

216

215

213 Butcher's Shop and original box, 1951. Tin and wooden back drop, wooden counter, trays of meat, scales, butcher with cleaver and butcher's block, butcher's assistant with tray and two female customers.

214 Fish Shop and original box, 1951. Tinplate and die-cast fish fryer, wooden counter, 'Frying Tonight' sign, assistant and two customers. The set also contained minute fish and chips.

215 Milk Bar or Ice Cream Parlour and original box, 1951. The same tinplate backdrop is used with the barber's shop set with added basins. Children on three high stools sit at wooden counter with cups and saucers and various ice cream sundaes and cones. A large tea urn and refrigerator together with a sign advertising 'Minerals and Ices' complete the set.
(Courtesy Helen and Martin Fahie)

216 Barber's Shop, 1951. Barber shaving customer, tin backdrop with wash basins and mirror.

251

HALBERD CASTINGS

Preston, 1952

Boxes containing Phillip Segal Products have come to light containing Nigerian rifles and Russian cossacks. It was reported in the January 1952 issue of *Games and Toys* that Halberd Castings were put in the hands of the official receiver. Upon advertising the disposal of Halberd's assets, almost the entire former Segal range was listed. Halberd had obviously bought up the moulds and finished Segal stock, but were not able to sustain their operations in the competitive toy world of the early 1950s.

252

HANKS BROTHERS

London, 1897

The brothers were former Britains employees who set up in opposition during the early 1900s. At first, in common with other Britains competitors, most of their products were direct copies of Britains figures. However, they did issue many original models in later years and it is believed that the firm ceased during the depression. An association with a Mr Sutton took place around this time and although unsuccessful, did provide collectors with the excellent Zulu with movable arm pictured in the Hanks section. Figures marked 'Sutton' occasionally come to light suggesting that Mr Sutton was also a manufacturer in his own right at some time.

251 Examples of men at arms in 40mm scale produced by Greenwood in the 1930s.

252 An advertisement published in *Games and Toys*, October 1914, confirming the partnership of Hanks and Sutton.

253 Box containing Hanks' copies of Britains Grenadier Guards with a Britains box for comparison. Hanks advertised and included one extra figure in each of their imitation sets produced in 1916.
(Courtesy James Opie)

253

254

All products date from 1916.

Top row: painted and gilt Camel Corps figures thought to have been manufactured by Hanks Brothers for Abel. The Lancer was one of the figures pirated by Hanks from the Britains range. Four 70mm figures: Red Indian chief, khaki peak cap at the slope, a rare infantry of the line (arm missing) and a Boy Scout with pole.

2nd row: copy of a Britains Guards officer, guardsmen at the trail and slope, infantry of the line and Worcester Regiment at the trail, fixed arm guardsman, infantry of the line, Highlander, khaki peak cap, two kneeling to receive cavalry figures, infantry of the line and khaki peak cap.

3rd row: the first two items are marked 'Sutton' on the underside of the base, the Zulu with movable arm is marked Hanks & Sutton. The others are all Hanks products: Boy Scout at attention with pole, Scoutmaster and Scout with movable arms, Scout with two movable arms, possibly to hold the handles of a trek cart, a rare trio of running Zulus.

255 *page 131* **Harvey military and cowboy and Indian figures, 1950**
Top row: Indian brave, Indian chief pointing, Indian running with tomahawk, chief kneeling firing bow and arrow, mounted cowboy firing two pistols, cowboy clubbing with rifle, cowboy with lasso, cowboy with two pistols, cowboy kneeling firing. Although none of the Harvey range bear any identifying marks, the horse has the letter 'H' under the saddle.

2nd row: Guards bandsmen, drum major, side drum, fife cymbals, bugle, Guards officer drawn sword, guardsman at ease, standing firing, slope arms, present arms.

3rd row: Red Berets standing firing, grenade thrower, kneeling firing and advancing with fixed bayonet, Highlanders side drummer, officer, piper and marching slope arms.

4th row: before Harvey left Crescent and formed his own company, he designed the items pictured here. The noticeable difference is that each guardsman has a pronounced crease cast into his trousers, guardsman slope arms and firing automatic weapon; three Indian chiefs, the first are original figures, the third an adaptation of the item top row, second left. The adapted figure's head-dress is indented rather than raised on the rear of his head.

256 Very rare boxed set of Harvey Indians distributed by DCMT, 1949. (Courtesy Mick Sharpe)

257 Metallic painted knights by H R Products, possibly formerly made by Pixyland, 1951. (Courtesy James Opie)

258 Treasure Island Series by HR Products, 1951. 'Famous Pirates – Fact and Fiction', Cutty Carver, Captain Hook, Black Jack with detachable dagger in mouth, Long John Silver and Wall Eye Jim.

256

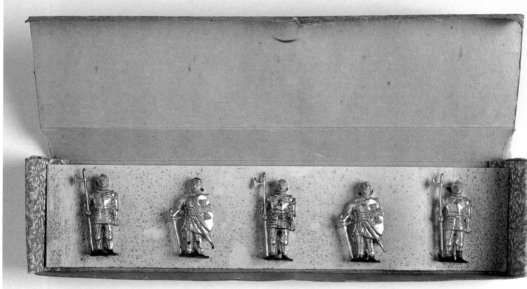

257

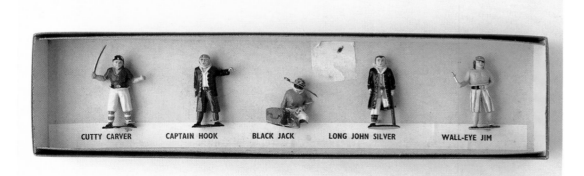

CUTTY CARVER   CAPTAIN HOOK   BLACK JACK   LONG JOHN SILVER   WALL-EYE JIM

258

HARVEY

London, 1949–1951

Harvey was founded by Harry Eagles son of Henry G Eagles, co-founder of Crescent. Harry Eagles had been known by the nickname Harvey and this name was used as the new company trade name. When Henry G Eagles died in 1942, Harry (Harvey) continued to work for Crescent after his discharge from the army. In 1949, when Crescent moved to South Wales, Harry Eagles remained in London, setting up the firm of Harvey in the north of the city. Many Harvey items resemble Crescent products. The firm only traded for a few years and Eagles later sold his trade name and designs to Lone Star (The Die-cast Metal Tool Co.) who introduced many of his figures into their range of plastics and renamed them 'Harvey Series'.

H R PRODUCTS

Fulham, London, 1951–1953

H R Products or Reynolds was started by a European immigrant named John Zanger. The company name was that of his son Harry Reynolds who employed R N Tooth on occasions to produce moulds for hollow-cast toy figures. Mr Tooth was a designer who also worked for Timpo, thus many of the figures issued by Reynolds resemble the products of Timpo. Mr Tooth has produced much of the information on many of the London firms producing figures in the 1950s and recalls one occasion when he was invited to Reynolds works in Farm Lane, Fulham, to meet Michael Bentine in order to design a set of the comedian's comic creations – The Bumblies.

259

Top row: Vikings: with axe above head, drawing sword, with axe at side, chief with winged helmet (rare light blue cape version), with dagger.
2nd row: Roman centurion, Viking in rare dark blue cape drawing sword, in rare green cape with axe at side, chief with sword (one wing on helmet missing) and Roman legionnaire.
3rd row: police directing traffic in blue and in white coat, mounted policeman, policeman on point duty and standing with hands behind back.

All figures date to 1951.

260

The Bumblies, 1951, were modelled after the comedian Michael Bentine's creations and are very rare.

JOHN HILL & CO (JOHILLCO)

London, 1898–1939, Burnley, 1946–1960s

John Hill & Company was established in 1898. It is not known how the company name was derived. The founder Mr F H Wood had been associated with the toy trade previously, having been an employee of William Britain. The firm's premises were situated at 2–22 Britannia Row, Islington, London N1. Few pre-World War I facts are known and similarly pre-World War I products are very difficult to find and identify as no catalogue for this early period has yet been found. After suspending production during part of the war, Hill became prolific in their output up to World War II.

Over 400 staff were employed in 1932, these being deployed in twelve departments – Designing and Modelling Room, Die and Mould Making Shop, Stamping and Press Shop, Metal Refining Plant, Trimming and Assembling Plant, Moulding and Casting Foundry, Process Painting Room, Carding, Boxing and Parcelling, Printing, Home and Export Packaging, Stock and Box Stock Rooms, Showrooms and Offices. Hills were self-sufficient and relied on no sub-contracting, as well as offering a casting service to others. This would account for boxed sets of Indians which have been found marked 'Perrins'.

As well as a wide range of lead figures, Hill also produced advertising and novelty items. Brooches depicting the FA Cup and signs of the zodiac, as well as souvenirs for the 1937 Coronation in the shape of crowns were produced. A large scale King George VI in coronation robes and seated on the Coronation Chair accompanied by a standing Queen Elizabeth was also made for the 1937 Coronation along with several boxed display sets containing the coach. By this time Hill had become the manufacturer that was only second in quality and quantity to Britains Limited. This was probably due to the wide variety of models which in the main were designed by Wilfred Cherrington (see Cherilea). In common with other manufacturers, production was suspended during World War II when the factory was bombed. However, most of the moulds were saved and these were subsequently shipped to Burnley in preparation for the commencement of post-war production.

In August 1946, John Hill & Co. (Metal Toys Ltd) was taken over by Mr Alec Standing of Burnley. Mr Standing operated a printing business at Burnley Wood Mill and used the trade name 'Alstan (Regd) Products Ltd'. His associates and partners in this venture were his brother Jim Standing, Jack Cooper and Gerry Cutts. The company name was changed slightly and became John Hill & Co. Metal Toy Manufacturers, retaining the John Hill name.

The Burnley factory opened in Plumbe Street, although the major part of Hill's operation moved to Parliament Street after the Plumbe Street premises became too small. Towards the end of production in the 1960s the firm operated from Ryland Street.

Hill employed local labour in their Burnley factories as well as 'out painters' who were needed during the height of the firm's production in the early 1950s. In order to advise on the casting and production of the figures, Jack Score was also employed in Burnley. Mr Score had worked for Hills before the war and had been associated with Wilfred Cherrington in designing figures. Tom Smith, a local man, was the foreman caster and with the help of Jack Score selected the necessary moulds.

The directors of the new firm obviously only wanted to market figures which were going to produce good sales. The old favourite lines were the first to be chosen and produced. Cowboys, Indians, guardsmen, knights, farm and zoo animals were in high demand and were churned out in their thousands as soon as enough raw material was released for toy production after the war.

The selection of moulds was not only based on marketable commodities, consideration also had to be given to the heat damaged moulds, and to the cost effectiveness of producing certain items. A good example is that of the horsedrawn cattle wagon which, although undamaged was thought too costly to produce post-war. Therefore, it must be assumed that the majority of pre-war issues which were not reissued post-war were rejected either because the figures were not considered to be commercial propositions or because the moulds were heat damaged.

After interviewing several of Hill's former employees, including Mr Keith Bunting, Mr Harold Cumpstey and Mrs Dolores Brown, it transpired that several items were produced post-war that have not yet come to light. Perhaps the most startling discovery was that of the educational 'ABC' Set. Dolores Brown who had been employed by Hills from the early post-war days was asked to put forward suggestions to the management for a special line to be supplied exclusively to 'Maceys' department store in New York. This set consisted of a large card printed with the letter corresponding to the name of the item, i.e. C for cow etc. When it came to the letter Z a problem arose – no item in the Hill range started with Z. Although one would have thought 'zebra' the obvious choice, Hill had never produced a zebra so the word 'zany' was chosen and a clown designed. This clown held two balloons on a string and must be classed as Hill's rarest item, bearing in mind that all were for export only and the set probably existed for only two or three years prior to Hill's demise.

261

Dated 1909, this movable arm, half-booted guardsman with moustache is one of the company's earliest products.

The top two boxes were probably issued prior to World War 1. The Abyssinian box probably contained the mountain mule battery. (Courtesy James Opie)

276

Pre-war gilt examples of the Hill khaki figures and a rare lion carrying the Union flag. A very rare mounted Russian is followed by Russian and Austro Hungarian infantry. (Courtesy James Opie)

Top row: two West Point cadets – bugler and slope arms (officer also available); US infantry in greatcoat with slung rifle; Royal Canadian Mounted Police – a sergeant, a mounted trooper and dismounted at ease; a rare movable arm US military policeman with baton; US marine at slope (bugler, officer and bulldog also issued); 47th New York Regiment at slope. Figures three, five and six issued pre- and post-war, the rest post-war only.

2nd row: Australian charging; Finnish ski troop; Greek Evzone (also issued in traditional white uniform); Japanese at slope and motor cycle with rider (both paint variations of khaki figures); Abyssinian tribesman with musket; Indian army in service dress, kneeling Zulu and a rare post-war version of the Zulu or Maori warrior. All pre-war except for last figure.

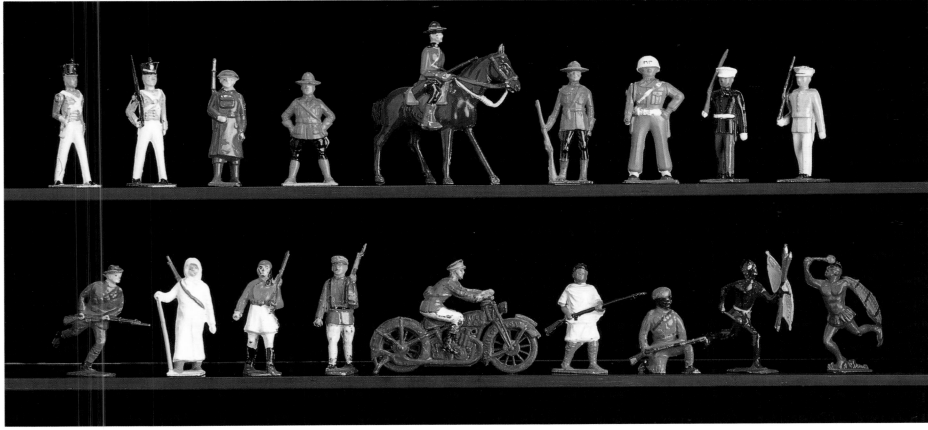

277

278

Top row: Arab in fez firing rifle, Sudanese Camel Corps, Arab with rifle raised above head. Issued pre- and post-war.
2nd row: two versions, painted and gilt of British Camel Corps listed by Hill as camels with riders. Elephant with mahout and rare early version of running elephant. All items pre-war only.

279 *page 147*
The five coloured 70mm figures were produced pre-war, but only the crusader with gold souvenir finish was available post-war. The figures comprise cowboy firing rifle, Indian chief and tomahawk, khaki peaked-cap officer, khaki soldier at the slope and crusader with sword and shield.

279

280

Top row: the mounted knight with movable lance arm and a lance which slots into the side of the horse to hold the arm upright, was issued pre- and post-war. The second knight was issued in 1955 as part of a newly-designed range by John Groom (as were figures three and five below). At right, two paint versions of the mounted crusader which were issued post-war.

2nd row: knights with movable arm in gold and silver; the feathered head-dress fighting knight is self-supporting by means of the scabbard at the back. The fourth figure is a knight with a morning star and shield followed by another fighting knight; two crusaders, both issued in 1955 (the first version is at far right). Items one, two and seven were issued both pre- and post war, the others are post-war only.

In 1951 the film 'Quo Vadis' starring Robert Taylor was released. Hill adapted their pre-war range of Romans, up-dated the paint style and issued this boxed set. The London department store Selfridges devoted a whole window to promote the sales of this item and it is therefore remarkable that the boxed set remains a rarity. A larger set also exists containing two chariots, additional Romans and a black panther. All of the animals are scaled down versions of those in the zoo range.

(Photograph courtesy Sue and Ian Toon)

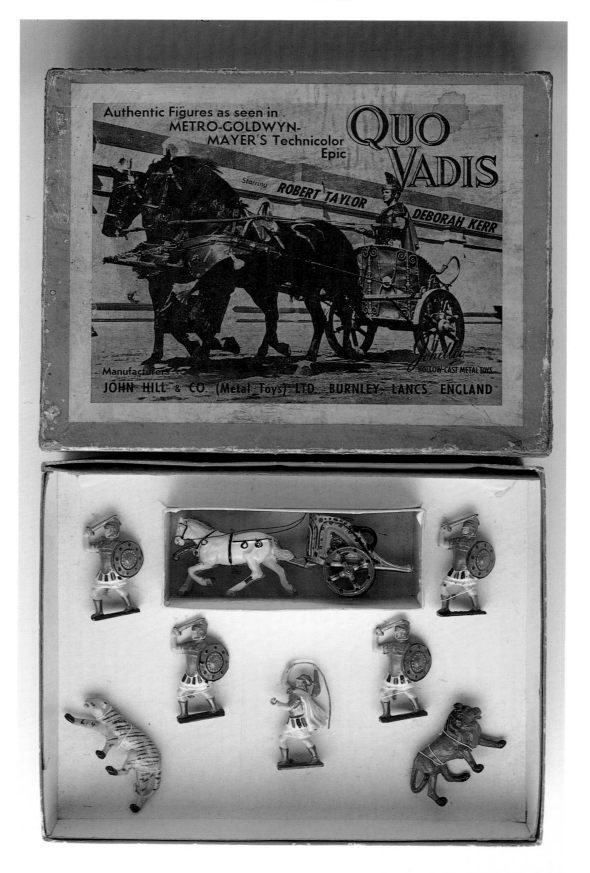

281

302

Top row: round and square haystacks, road signs with various warnings printed on paper stickers and a well. The square haystack was also produced in tin and is a rarity. Pre- and post-war.

2nd row: water pump, miniature cottage, wheatsheaves, very rare sign (adapted pre-war from railway station boards), two-section bridge and pigsty. All except cottage are post-war.

3rd row: fence with stile, gate fence, post- and pre-war version of cattle drinking bowl, covered seat (rare) and tinplate step ladder. All pre-war except for post-war cattle trough.

303

Top row: turkey, pecking chicken, rooster, hen coup, chicks in two positions, hen (black on nest), large open dovecote with pigeon and dove, hen (brown) on nest, small closed dovecote, pecking hen (brown), beehive and goat.

2nd row: lying sheep, lamb, pig, sleeping and sitting black piglets, sleeping, sitting and walking piglets, running pig, seated pig, lying pig, sheep standing and sheep feeding.

3rd row: collie dog, farm dog, rare angry gander, goose flapping wings, pond with swan and cygnet, ducks standing, swimming and walking, fox hound (listed by Hill as fox terrier) and lying dog.

All items post-war, except for the dovecote in top row which was available pre-war only.

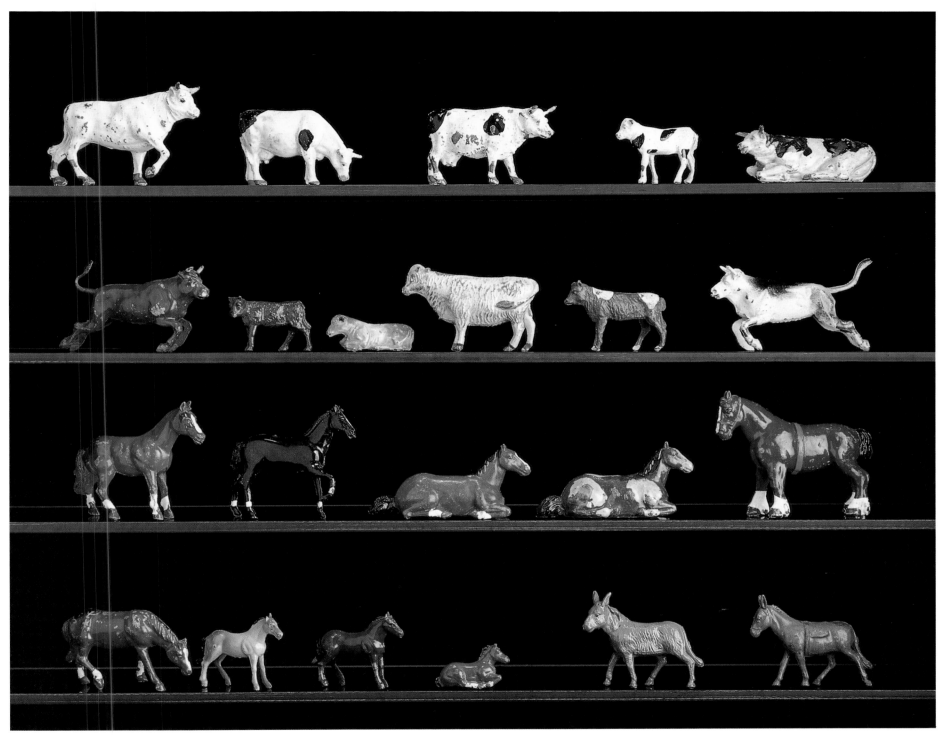

304

These examples of animals from the farm range are all fairly common, except for the Highland cow (row two) with its tail cast into its body and the stallion (third row, second left). Both were issued for only a short period after World War II. All other items available pre- and post-war.

Top row: English bull, feeding cow, cow, calf, lying cow.
2nd row: two paint versions of running steer, Highland calf, lying calf, Highland cow, shaggy calf.
3rd row: horse, stallion, two variations of lying horse, shire-horse.
4th row: feeding horse, two variations of foal, lying colt, donkey, mule.

305

Top row: three examples of the farmer, probably the most common civilian item produced. It turns up in boxed Timpo sets and was also issued by Fylde and Crescent. The third example has been painted as a huntsman. Seated drover with handkerchief, old lady, three paint versions of the shepherd carrying a lamb.
2nd row: rabbit hutch and rabbits, bull dog and kennel with 'Beware of the Dog' sign, and three milkmaids — carrying yoke, seated on three-legged stool (issued as farmer's daughter) and seated milking.
3rd row: drover with red rag and stick, gardener in floppy hat pushing barrow, very rare market gardener with tray of produce, man pushing wheelbarrow (also issued in grey to complement the Millers Series), country curate with bible, inn keeper and tramp.

All available pre- and post-war, except item three 3rd row pre-war only.

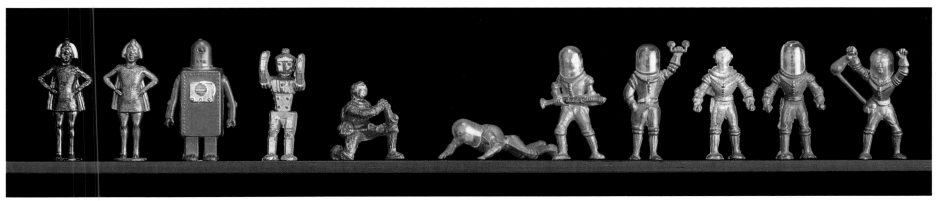

325

326

327

A selection of space men and aliens c.1950, designed by Wilfred Cherrington for Hill and most later reissued by Cherilea. The figures not reissued, and therefore rare, are the purple-coloured robot and the spaceman fourth from right. A series of wooden space stations were also released by John Hill in 1953.

Boxes exported post-war to the United States were amongst Hill's most colourful. The box marked 'Buckingham' was specially designed for Macy's department store.

Example of post-war box lid for the United States.
(Photograph courtesy Christies, South Kensington)

328 Kay were not renowned as manufacturers, but this wooden zoo sign may have been made by them to complement a boxed set containing Taylor & Barrett zoo animals.

329 Although Kay were responsible for packaging other companies' products, these illustrated sets and box artwork suggest they may also have been manufacturers. (Cowboy and Indian box lid and boxed zoo set containing Taylor & Barrett products are courtesy of Helen and Martin Fahie.) The hospital set is by an unknown manufacturer and is very rare.

330 Examples of the packaging used for Keymen footballers in 1966. Perspex-fronted box containing 'The International Four' – Bobby Charlton, Colin Bell, Alan Ball and Bobby Moore. Billy Bremner in the colours of Leeds United and Martin Peters in the Tottenham Hotspur strip. Second version box containing Colin Bell in Manchester City colours and first version box containing Gordon Banks, the England goalkeeper, in yellow jersey.

331 Shop display stand for Keymen figures: George Best with ball, (Manchester United), Colin Bell (England), Alan Ball (Everton), Bobby Moore (West Ham United), Francis Lee (Manchester City), Gordon Banks (Leicester City) and Bobby Charlton (Manchester United), 1966. (Courtesy Helen and Martin Fahie)

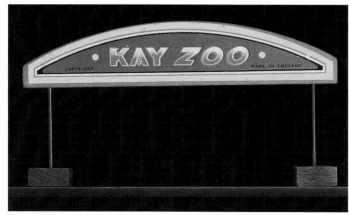

328

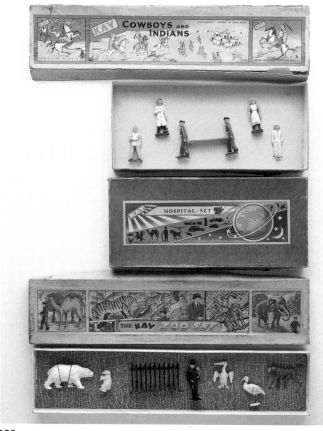

329

330

KAY

London, 1936–1958

Kay were a packaging company who, before the war, boxed the products of Taylor & Barrett and Charbens into display sets. Two items exist that perhaps indicate that Kay employed others to manufacture on their behalf. One is a petrol pump and the other, a wooden sign displaying the words 'Kay Zoo', was included in boxes of T & B zoo animals and keepers. Barrett & Sons entered into an agreement post-World War II for Kay to issue flock-coated animals supplied by the firm of Laing. Barrett & Sons marketed these items under the brand name of 'Fur-E-Toys'. The boxed hospital set illustrated in a Kay box contains figures by an as yet unidentified manufacturer.

KEYMEN

Liverpool, 1966

The manufacturer of Keymen footballers is not known. Keymen was a trade name only. The figures were die-cast and 60mm in height. The name Keymen was derived from the fact that the models were painted by prisoners in Liverpool prison. The range consisted of many well known football personalities whose careers were at their height around the time of the 1966 World Cup.

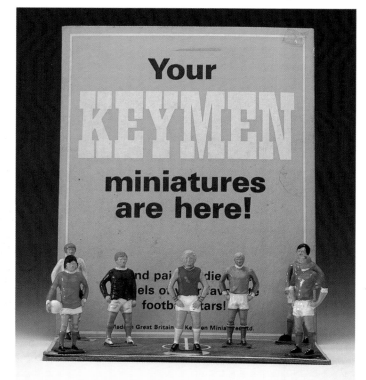

331

LAING PRODUCTS

London, 1948

Subcontracted by the following firms:

Sacul Pixyland/Kew
Wend-Al John Hill & Co.
Timpo Barrett & Sons

Laing specialised in flock-coating and was based in Ealing. Examples have been found among the ranges of figures produced by the above companies. Most flock-coating was applied to animals. The exception being the busbies of Timpo guardsmen and trees sold by John Hill & Co. Sacul guardsmen were also given the flock busby treatment.

LAURIE

London, 1916

Nothing is known of this firm other than the advertisement shown below.

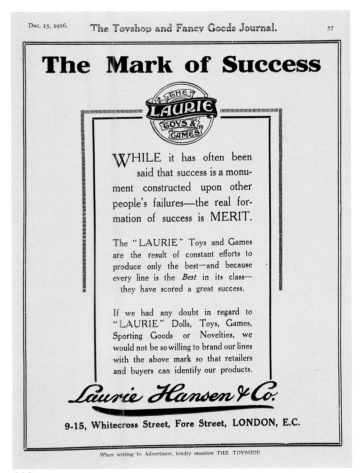

332

333

334

335

LORD ROBERTS WORKSHOPS

London, 1916

Providing work and rehabilitation for disabled ex-servicemen during World War I, Lord Roberts' and Lord Kitchener's Workshops released lead figures probably manufactured by either Fry, Hanks or one of the other smaller companies who existed during the period.

332 Advertisement from the *Toyshop and Fancy Goods Journal*, December 1916.

333 Prior to the discovery of this boxed set, no Laurie toy soldiers had come to light. Although crude, these pipers are of original design and date to 1916.
(Courtesy Bill Kingsman)

334 Charging Scottish figures in Glengarry and feather bonnet and London Scottish variations by Lord Roberts' Workshops, 1916.
(Courtesy Jim Lloyd)

335 Charging highlander and very rare running piper by Lord Roberts' Workshops, 1916.
(Courtesy James Opie)

336 The Luntoy children's television character range, designed and manufactured by Barrett & Sons in 1952, was issued in boxes representing television sets: Prudence Kitten, Peregrin Penguin, Princess Tai Liu (Siamese cat) with tiara, Sooty playing the xylophone, Muffin the Mule and Mr Turnip.

337 The Luntoy figures of Rag (hedgehog), Tag (mouse) and Bobtail (rabbit) are only about one quarter the size of similar examples illustrated in the Sacul section. Billy Bean and two versions of Hank on Silver King, the first being the standard issue, the second recast from a prototype mould which was not put into production and is therefore unique. Finally, Andy Pandy and a Flowerpot Man, 1952.

338 String puppets manufactured by Barrett & Sons for Luntoy in 1953. A Flowerpot Man was the only other character issued in this series.

336

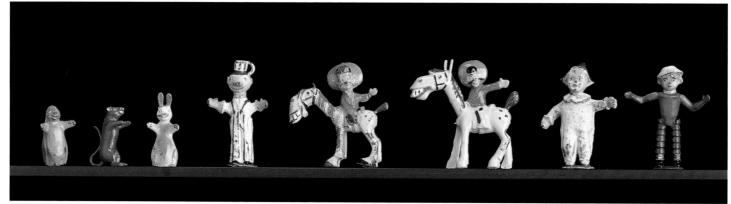

337

338

LUNTOY

London, 1950–1954

TV characters were designed and manufactured for the London Toy Company by Barrett & Sons. Barrett produced and boxed these popular early BBC children's TV characters. Luntoy had previously issued wooden forts and seized the opportunity to cash in on these children's favourites. Large die-cast string puppets depicting Mr Turnip, Flowerpot Man and Sooty were also produced by Barrett & Sons.

Upon the termination of trading, Barrett & Sons and Luntoy entered into an agreement to buy up the remaining Sacul moulds. Barrett & Sons manufactured and packaged knights from the former Sacul range. Some later mounted knights bear a marked resemblance to Timpo and are marked 'Paramount'. The difference can be seen by comparing these with the standard range of knights illustrated in the Sacul section.

362

65mm figures

Top row: rare policeman with truncheon in movable arm pursuing burglar with cosh and lamp; butcher with side of beef and knife by Pixyland; Kew figure of a butcher with knife and monk. At right the underside of the monk's base shows the Kew label and trade mark 'Kuzad'.

2nd row: postman with letter, postman with movable arm, fireman with axe and lamp and policeman in overcoat. These figures were advertised in 1922 (see below).

Advertisement from *Games and Toys*, 1922. The children's pets were Pip, Squeak and Wilfred (see **359**).

FIREMEN, POLICEMEN, BURGLARS, RAILWAY GUARDS, BUTCHERS, POSTMEN, RED RIDING HOOD, BOY BLUE, CAT & FIDDLE, &c.

FATHER XMAS.   HUNTING SETS.

PIXYLAND TOYS

THE CHILDREN'S PETS.

DOES YOUR WHOLESALER STOCK THESE LINES?

PIXYLAND TOY & MANUFACTURING Co., 22½, Cazenove Road, Stoke Newington, N.16.

363

364

All items are rare except the figure at far left in row two and date to the pre-war period.
Top row: farmer with shotgun and dog; seated and standing ale drinkers with movable arms holding foaming tankards; man and wheelbarrow, old lady in shawl and old man with stick.
2nd row: tramp, unpainted casting of a man holding a cudgel or bladder (which I suggest is possibly the ultra rare Kew 'village fool'. The name probably derived from the Morris dancing team which would have contained a 'fool' with balloon or bladder); landgirl with bucket; scarecrow; milkmaid with two removable buckets; girl with basket feeding hens, and probably the most common Kew item – farmer with removable pitchfork.
3rd row: nanny holding baby, town crier, man in dungarees with cloth, petrol cart, man with petrol can, 'Pratts' petrol can and chimney sweep.

Kew Hunt Series

Post-war these moulds were taken over by Timpo and issued in their boxes entitled 'Happy Hunting Series'. Two versions of the 'whip' are illustrated at right. The example with outstretched horse's tail is probably the Pixyland version issued prior to 1932.

365

This rare complete set with 45 mm figures was sold as part of Kew's 'Oval Cricket Game', 1928.

366

367

Pixyland Noah and animals

This set produced c.1930 was probably not reissued by Kew after taking over Pixyland. The scale of the figures is variable.

Top row: giraffe, camel, mountain goat, Noah, baby elephant, gibbon and ostrich.

2nd row: cow, ram, dog with outstretched tail, auk or albatross and horse.

3rd row: hippopotamus, tiger, brown bear, polar bear, wallaby and lion.

368 *page 187*

The top three rows contain fairly common pieces including, on the top row, four bulls in different positions. The fourth figure in row three is a rare wild sheep.

4th row: the arched black cat second left and the owl and rat, third and fourth left, are rare items, while most of the rest are fairly easily identifiable and obtainable.

All figures are pre-war.

368

384

385

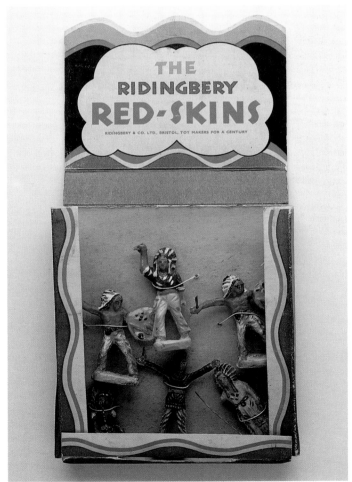

386

384 RACO farm animals and soldiers from c.1934.
Top row: foal, sheep, ram, ewe, donkey, hen, pig, goat and dog (the latter issued in the Red Riding Hood set as the wolf).
2nd row: seven guardsmen – bugler, tuba, cymbals, trombone, fife, marching bugler, at the slope; infantry of the line bugler, infantryman charging fixed bayonet, miniature mounted Life Guard, Horse Guard and Life Guard.

385 Rare boxed set by RACO containing characters from Little Red Riding Hood: wolf, tree, woodman, wolf dressed as granny in bed and Little Red Riding Hood. The story is printed inside the box lid. All figures date to c.1934.

386 Boxed set of Ridingbery composition Red Indians, 1952.
(Courtesy Helen and Martin Fahie)

387

ROYDON

Wallasey, Cheshire, 1949–1952

Operating from Wallasey in Cheshire during the early 1950s, Roydon issued a series of farm figures and are known to have advertised military items. None of these have yet come to light, but may be among the many unidentified items shown in the last section (pages 262-267). Some of the farm pieces may have been manufactured for them by John Hill & Co.

388

389

387 *Top row:* signpost, windmill, man pushing barrow, well and bird house.
2nd row: cow, goat, dog and milkmaid with two buckets.
All items date to 1949.

388 Box label for the Home Farm set, 1949.

389 Rare blacksmith set with separate tools, 1949.

RUSSELL MANUFACTURING CO

London, 1908

Russell Manufacturing Company existed until the out-break of World War I. Identification is made easy by the distinctive numbering under the base of each figure. British infantry regiments formed the main part of a small range. Boxed sets have been found marked R M & Co and Briyta. As well as a Boy Scout, Russell are known to have issued footballers with wire attached to movable legs and, in the goalkeeper's case, arms, to give the desired effect of kicking legs or moving arms.

Infantry of the line officer and two versions of the slope arms figure; Royal Marine officer and man; Highlanders in Glengarry and tropical uniform; guardsmen firing and at slope; Rifle Brigade, RMLI, khaki steel helmet officer and man, Sikh at attention and footballer whose leg is operated by a wire. All figures date from 1908.

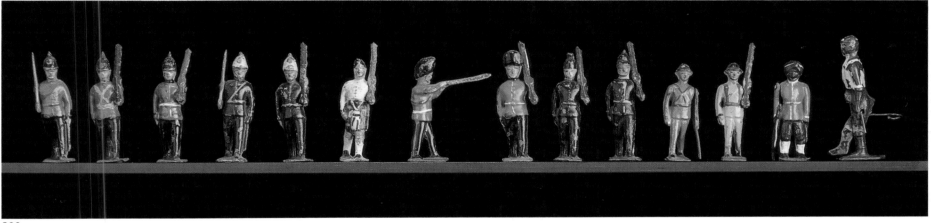

390

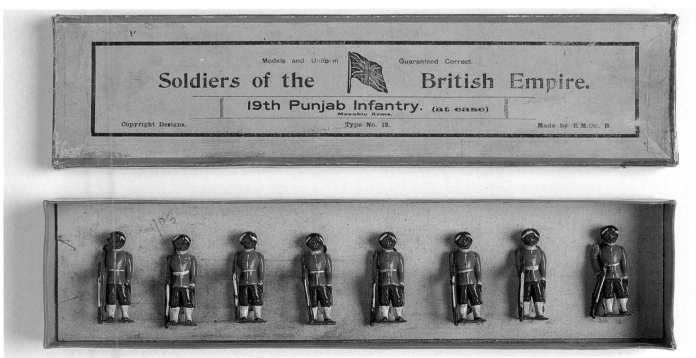

391

This rare boxed set containing the 19th Punjab infantry at ease with movable arms is marked 'R M and Co' and dates to 1908. (Courtesy James Opie)

Games and Toys advertisement, 1953, showing the full range of the rare Sacul Disney characters.

SACUL

Forest Gate, London, 1951–1954

Sacul was owned by a former employee of Timpo who reversed his own name (Lucas) to form a trade name. Sacul operated in London in the 1950s and at first issued cowboy suits for children. Many of Sacul's products were influenced by Timpo figures and were often enhanced by the addition of silver vacuum-coating. Knights with movable visors are thought to have been devised first by Lucas. A Barrett & Sons also had a hand in assisting and producing masters for Lucas. Large size children's TV characters as well as Disney figures were also introduced. The quality of Sacul products was excellent. However the firm was to be short lived. Mr Lucas, after becoming insolvent, re-emerged under the name Paramount to concentrate on his previous success with the novel chrome-plated knights. Again this venture was doomed as the hollow-cast fell from favour and plastic took over.

393

Walt Disney figures of Pluto, Mickey and Minnie Mouse, 1953. Both mice have wire tails and Pluto has a detachable collar. Donald Duck and Goofy were included in the range. All are very rare.

394

Flowerpot Men, Bill and Ben, Weed and original terracotta flower pots and box, 1951.

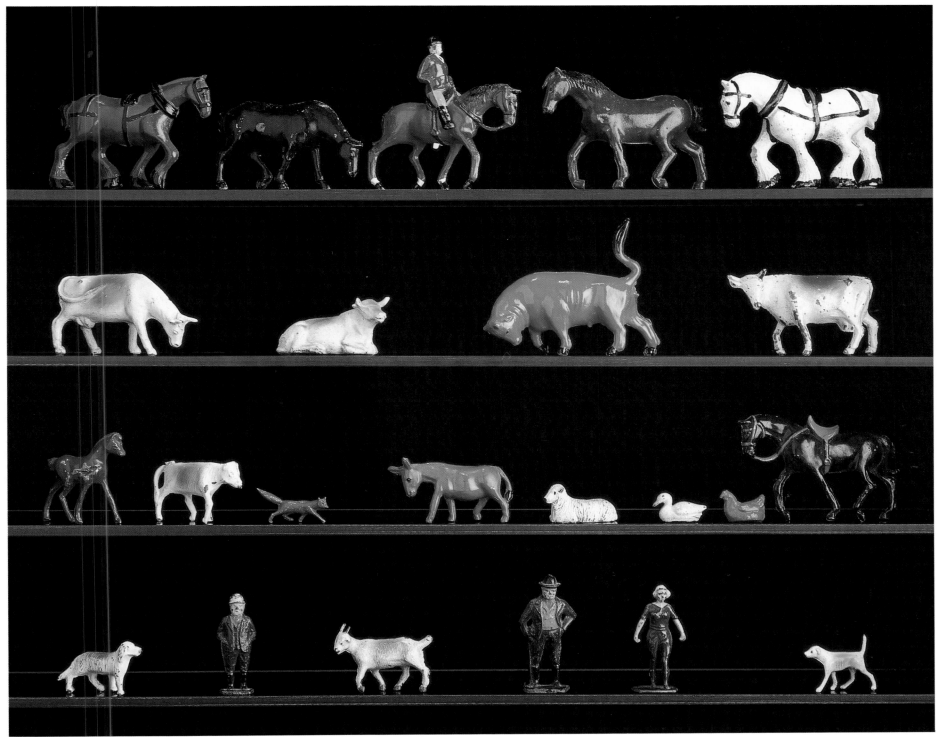

417

Farm animals, c.1949
Top row: shire-horse, horse feeding, very rare mounted gentleman farmer
(courtesy Ian and Sue Toon), field horse and white shire-horse.
2nd row: feeding and lying cows, very rare bull (courtesy Roger Maryon)
and cow with turned head.

3rd row: foal, calf, fox, donkey, lying sheep, swimming duck, sitting hen,
and racehorse with saddle.
4th row: dog, farmer, goat, larger scale farmer, Women's Land Army girl,
capable of holding two buckets, and hound.

418

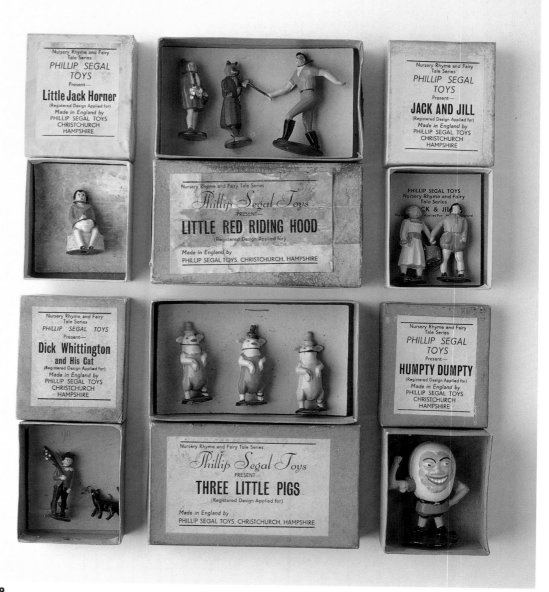

419

This 1949 export catalogue illustrates the Nursery Rhyme and Fairy Tale Series and reveals a set not known to exist. 'Hey Diddle Diddle the Cat and the Fiddle' does not bear a patent number and was probably never issued. (Courtesy Pam and Bill Brunton)

419 Boxed examples of the Nursery Rhyme and Fairy Tale Series, produced for only about one year – 1949–1950.
Top row: Little Jack Horner, Little Red Riding Hood, Wolf in Granny's clothes and woodman, Jack and Jill with looped hands holding bucket.
Bottom row: Dick Whittington and his Cat, the Three Little Pigs and Humpty Dumpty.

420 Nursery rhyme and fairy tale figures, c.1949: the Three Bears and Goldilocks, the Old Woman's Shoe with three children and the Old Woman and Little Bo Peep with sheep.

420

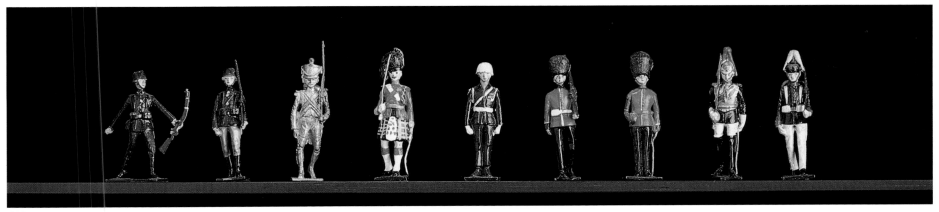

421

STADDEN

London, 1949 – present day

Best known for and still producing military miniatures, Charles Stadden issued a small range of 'toy' soldiers in solid lead during the late 1950s. The figures appear only to have been for sale via Norman Newton's retail outlet in the Shepherd's Market area of London.

STODDART

London, 1916–1939

Stoddart soldiers were issued in boxes marked 'Wellington Series', while a range of babies, children, zoo and farm animals were available, loose in bulk packs. Upon the outbreak of World War II Stoddart ceased production and did not resume toy making after the war. Many of the Stoddart moulds were purchased by Timpo and were included in Timpo boxed sets between 1946 and 1950.

422

421 Nine figures from Stadden's short-lived toy soldier range: German World War II grenade thrower with rifle; German slope arms with movable arm; unpainted French Napoleonic troop; Gordon Highlander officer; US Army Honour Guard; guardsman marching at slope, Guards officer at attention with drawn sword, Horse Guards officer and Chilean Ceremonial Guard. All c.1950.

422 Advertisement from *Games and Toys*, September 1916.

423 Rare seated Negro children's jazz band and various babies, c.1920 by Stoddart.

424 Very rare early Stoddart Mickey Mouse, 1932.

423

424

425

Many of the Stoddart items
illustrated were bought by Timpo
between 1946 and 1950.
Top row: elephant, camel, giraffe,
gorilla, deer, doe, leopard, lion, goat
and donkey.
2nd row: cowboy with rifle and
cowboy surrendering, six
guardsmen – standing firing, bugler,
slope, attention, side drummer and
at the ready.

TAG

London, 1951

60mm composition military figures bearing a cardboard
tag tied to the figure. The tag contained information on
the history of the regiment and the firm sold them under
the guise of educational toys.

Plaster composition educational toys
issued by Tag during the mid-1950s.

426

TAYLOR & BARRETT

London, 1920–1984

Founded in 1920 by brothers A R Barrett, S Barrett and F G Taylor. The firm started producing on a part time basis, working evenings and supplying 'cast lead toys' direct to Charbens and a number of toy shops. The Barrett brothers had been employed by William Britain Ltd as casters, during the pre-World War I period. S Barrett left the partnership in the early 1920s, but was re-employed at a later date by the remaining two partners.

The business was operated from a mews building in Scholfield Road, Upper Holloway, North London. Working conditions were primitive and consisted of wooden floored buildings, open lead melting pots and little ventilation. Five-gallon paint drums were situated in the same room, and the finished products were dipped and laid out on wooden trays to dry.

In 1923 the partners decided that business was good enough to enable them to start producing on a full time basis. B S Barrett, in his summary of the firm's history, written in 1984, mentions that the first models to be produced were a very large camel, governess cart and pony, a Zulu/Chinaman to pull a rickshaw, two Indians paddling a canoe and a large elephant and howdah. Moulds for these early T & B figures were made in the same room as the above listed activities. After the model had been made a plaster of paris mould would be made. These were then cast in aluminium and after experimenting in home-made sand boxes, usable moulds were made. These were mounted on soft iron tongs and bandaged at the ends with rags to enable the caster to hold the mould. The trimming was carried out by boys, employed part time, while the wives of the partners and paid outworkers took care of the painting work.

In 1928 Barrett's eldest son Alfred left school and joined the firm as a trainee caster. By 1929 the business had outgrown the Scholfield Road premises and a purpose-built factory was rented in East Finchley, North London. The national slump of the 1930s nearly ended the enterprise on several occasions. However, the storm was weathered and the firm survived. 1934 saw Bert, the second Barrett son leave school and join his father, brother, uncle and nine or ten casters. Bert Barrett learned the basics for a year or so before concentrating on mould-making. The method had changed slightly as now the plaster casts were sent to a foundry to be cast in brass. The castings were rough and needed a great deal of work to restore the detail.

During the 1930s, A Barrett (senior) was responsible for the business side by supervising the workshops, which consisted of a casting and trimming shop, an assembly department, a packaging department, a spray shop and approximately twenty female painters. Mr Taylor supervised the mould room where Bert Barrett worked. Up to 1940 large ranges of motor cars, fire engines, zoo and farm animals, soldiers and dolls' house furniture were produced. Bert Barrett entered the army in 1939 at which time most Taylor & Barrett products were going to the export market.

Materials were becoming difficult to obtain and the production was running down when, in 1940, the East Finchley factory was gutted in an air raid. All that could be salvaged was transported to a larger factory in North Finchley. The production here was short lived and it was not long before the government decided that munitions and not toys should be the main objective. The firm closed, the stock was sold and the moulds divided for safe keeping between F G Taylor and A R Barrett. During 1945 both A R Barrett and his son Alfred were released from war work and were keen to restart the business. Mr Taylor was approached, but differences of opinion and family commitments prevented the partnership from being revived.

Two companies were then formed. F G Taylor and his son Fred Taylor junior, and Fred Taylor senior's son-in-law Fred Squires formed a company trading as F G Taylor & Sons with the trademark 'For Good Toys'. It is believed that this company was still in existence in 1978. The Barretts formed A Barrett & Sons. Bert was released from the army and joined his father and brother in 1946. F G Taylor & Sons operated from 22 Hampden Road, London N19, while the Barretts traded from Sonderburg Road, London N7.

Kay Packaging
Taylor & Barrett items were supplied to Kay who were packaging/display box distributors. Barrett & Sons continued to supply Kay with flock-coated animals post-war.

C E Turnbull (Cetandco)
Also issued some Taylor & Barrett horse-drawn vehicles pre-war.

T & B governess cart with four children and llama cart ride, c. 1930. The llama ride at right is a post-war Barrett & Sons issue with a new llama.

Top row: pre-war T & B camel ride and two post-war Barrett & Sons rides (the right hand item being plastic).
2nd row: nine T & B pre-war figures. The first three described as 300 visitors; twins hand in hand; seated man and woman from 'Zoo visitors at tea' set, as is the waitress. The parrots are post-war Taylor & Sons issues.

449

450

451

Taylor & Barrett, c.1930

Top row: three giraffes, the first two the same second version casting, the second flock-coated and the third an early first version; squirrel tree and ostrich; three versions of the kangaroo, the last flock sprayed.
2nd row: buffalo, hippopotamus, bison, stag, young elephant, rhinoceros.

3rd row: seated and walking polar bears, bear cubs, baboon with orange, climbing monkey, gorilla and tree, seated lioness and lion, walking lion and llama.
4th row: snake, eagle, pelican, stork, penguin, alligator, ass, gibbon, parrot and hyena.

Top row: two pre-war T & B pay
boxes (green part of the zoo items,
red part of a garage set); pre-war
zoo gate; post-war Taylor & Sons
reissued gate; post-war Barrett &
Sons reissued palm tree and Taylor
& Sons elephant steps.
2nd row: post-war railings, zoo pay
boxes, turnstiles and tree reissued
by Barrett & Sons.

453 A Barrett & Sons elephant ride
with new elephant issued in 1950.
This rare boxed example is a
transitional set comprising a lead
elephant and howdah with plastic
keeper and children.

454 A Barrett & Sons giant tortoise
ride and girl with original string, 1948.
(Courtesy Sue and Ian Toon)

452

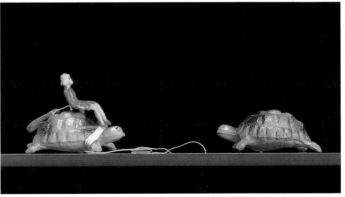

454

453

Two transitional Taylor & Sons sets using a combination of lead and plastic components, 1950. Elephant ride with lead howdah and chimpanzee tea party with lead table, chairs and keeper's bucket.

455

Top row: newly designed Taylor & Sons animals, walking and sitting polar bears and cub. The seated bear and cub were also issued as 'Ivy and Brumas' in a boxed set. Brown bear paint versions of the polar bears.
2nd row: Taylor & Sons walking camel, baby camel, kangaroo, lioness and tiger.

All date to 1950.

456

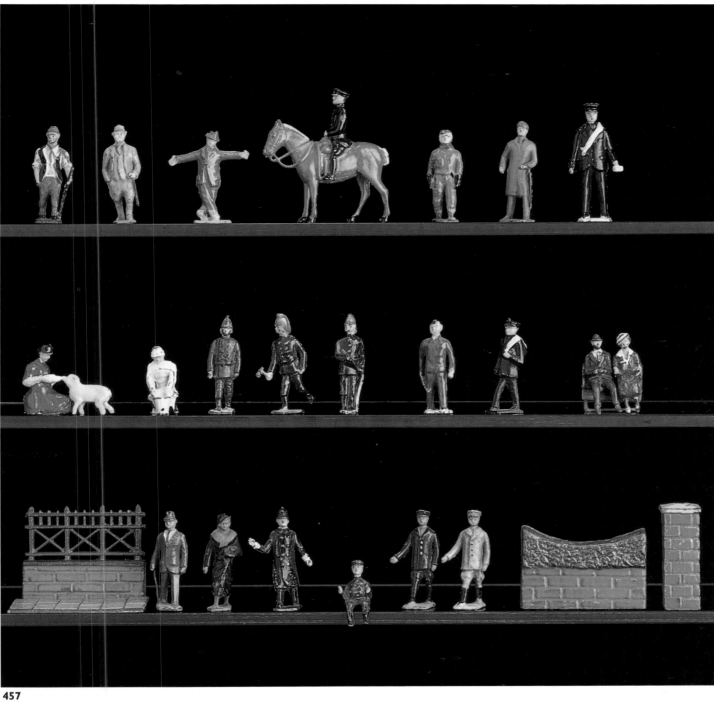

With the exception of the Barrett & Sons postman in the top row, and walls and brickwork pillars by T & B, all items are 40mm scale.

Top row: Taylor & Sons cowman (reissue of pre-war T & B figure); Barrett & Sons reissued farmer; Taylor & Sons new post-war scarecrow; reissued Barrett & Sons policeman; new Barrett & Sons pilot, man with umbrella and postman.

2nd row: Taylor & Sons reissued post-war maid feeding lamb, Barrett & Sons post-war reissue of seated milkmaid, policeman by T & B; two T & B firemen with axe and hose; Taylor & Sons reissued post-war mechanic; pre-war T & B postman and seated couple made for Minic cars.

3rd row: T & B pre-war wall section and pillar, man, woman, policeman and three pre-war T & B chauffeurs.

457

458

Top row: T & B and Taylor & Sons both issued the bellowing cow at left and the bull at right. Barrett & Sons issued the second standing cow to replace the bellowing cow. The lying cow at left and the grazing cow at right were made by both T & B and Barrett & Sons, while the lying cow at right is by Taylor & Sons, issued to replace the former lying cow inherited by Barrett & Sons.

2nd row: T & B uncatalogued feeding horse; second and fourth horses and wheatsheaf are post-war Taylor & Sons issues; light brown foal and dark mother and foal are post-war T & B reissues by Barrett & Sons.

3rd row: two post-war new goats by Barrett & Sons (the first flock-sprayed) with new Taylor & Sons goat (T & B did not issue a goat); Barrett & Sons Shetland pony and first calf with T & B pre-war calf; Barrett & Sons lying calf (a new issue as no lying calf produced pre-war); Taylor & Sons pecking hen; Barrett & Sons turkey, swan, cygnet and milkmaid.

4th row: Barrett & Sons post-war new issue standing and lying dogs and lamb; Taylor & Sons new issue chicks and ducks; first lying and grazing sheep and the two pigs produced by T & B and reissued post-war by Barrett & Sons; second lying and standing sheep by Taylor & Sons, the lying sheep a reissue to compensate for original model inherited by Barrett & Sons.

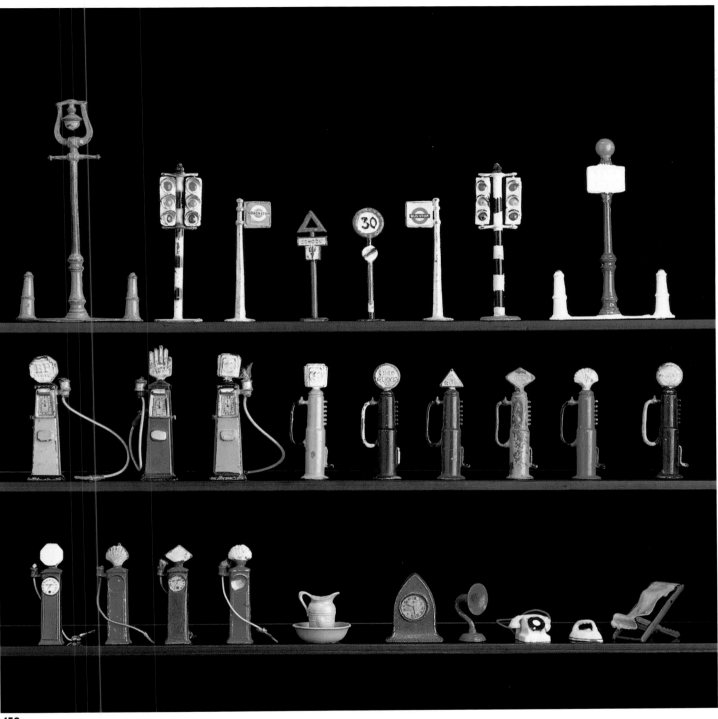

Top row: T & B traffic island with lamp, traffic lights, school and 30 mph signs; Taylor & Sons bus stops; Barrett & Sons safety island.
2nd row: T & B petrol pumps. The Ethyl hand pump is rare.
3rd row: T & B smaller scale petrol pumps, jug and basin, mantle clock, gramophone horn and rare deckchair, Barrett & Sons post-war telephone and iron.

Wild West

Top row: examples of individual boxes which contained the figures illustrated – mounted Indian chiefs with tomahawk, bow and shield.

2nd row: bandit, cowboy with rifle and pistol and firing rifle.

3rd row: cowboys mopping brow, hands raised in surrender, rifle raised and hands tied behind back.

4th row: cowboy with lasso chasing wild horse, cowboy with lasso, cowboy roping steer. All three examples of cowboy horses are illustrated.

All items date to 1950.

484

Wild West Series, 1950

Top row: sheriff; cowboy tied to wooden tree (second version of lead tree at right); seated cowboys playing accordian and guitar with campfire; Timpo Tim.

2nd row: cowboy dropping pistol, bandit with two pistols, mounted Royal Canadian Mounted Policeman, bandit firing and drawing pistol, cowboy with US mail bag.

3rd row: chief standing and running with spear, chief seated, Indian lying, 'scouting' squaw; three versions of seated brave with tom-tom (the first with shallow drum is quite scarce, the second with a deeper drum is illustrated in two colour variations).

4th row: braves standing and kneeling with bows and arrows, brave with raised hands, two colour variations of running brave with spear.

485

Zoo animals, 1950
Top row: giraffe, camel, hippopotamus, Indian water buffalo, rhinoceros, and elk or stag.
2nd row: baby elephant, sea-lion, kangaroo, monkey on tree, squirrel on branch, a flock-sprayed and standard issue zebra and ostrich.
3rd row: brown bear, standard and flock-sprayed polar bear, walking polar bear, brown bear cub, polar bear cub, black bear and brown bear walking. The walking polar bear and polar bear cub were also issued as 'Ivy and Brumas'.
4th row: tiger, lioness, lion, crocodile, penguin, eagle, pelican, stork, turtle and mountain goat or ibex.

Top row: zoo picture box which contained a cage, one animal, zoo inspector, zoo keeper sweeping with brush and cage.
2nd row: bison, keeper with two buckets and elephant with raised trunk.
All items date to 1950.

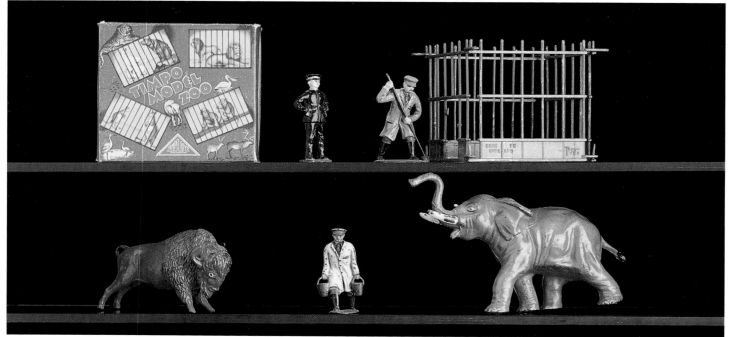

486

Timpo model zoo set in original box, 1950.
(Courtesy Helen and Martin Fahie)

487

488

Examples of mounted and foot knights issued in 1950 prior to the King Arthur and Ivanhoe ranges.

489

Ivanhoe and crusaders, 1951. Four sets of medieval figures based on feature films were produced by Timpo. Ivanhoe (The Black Knight) is illustrated in the centre with Ralph de Vimper and Bois de Guilbert at left. Three paint versions of the crusader were issued. The missing example wore a yellow surcoat and rode a horse wearing yellow and gold cloth.

US Army Series, 1950. The doctor is the railway passenger boy reissued in a white coat. About one in every ten GI figures were issued as black GIs, one of which may be seen at rear left with slung rifle. The complete range is illustrated, full descriptions of which appear in the inventory at the back of the book.

506

Tiger Hunt set with white hunter, Indian Rajah and beaters, 1950. The tiger at right was issued with a hole and protruding spear and Timpo added red paint to represent blood. The tiger at left is a very rare flock-sprayed example.

507

Railway passengers and station staff

Top row: Mrs Smith and Mr Smith said to have been based on the real-life Mr Selwyn Smith, who was most prolific in his designs for Timpo, and his wife; business man, lady holding little boy by hand, hiker, girl, Mr Brown, boy, commercial traveller and Mrs Green.

2nd row: station master, guard blowing whistle and waving green flag, guard with whistle, porter carrying four pieces of luggage, sailor with kit bag, soldier with slung rifle and kit bag, signalman with two lamps, luggage (a hat box was also part of this set), porter pushing two-wheel trolleys.

All items date to 1950.

508

Box for Timpo station figures, as issued to the US market in 1951. (Courtesy James Opie)

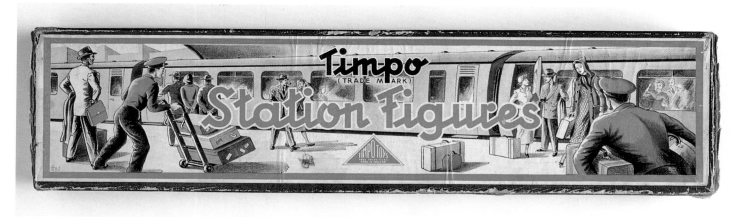

509

510 Rare paint variations of Mrs Green from the Railway Series, 1950. These items are thought to have been commissioned as fairground prizes.

511 Semi-flat 30mm railway items are rare as they were only produced for a short period between 1950 and 1951.

510

511

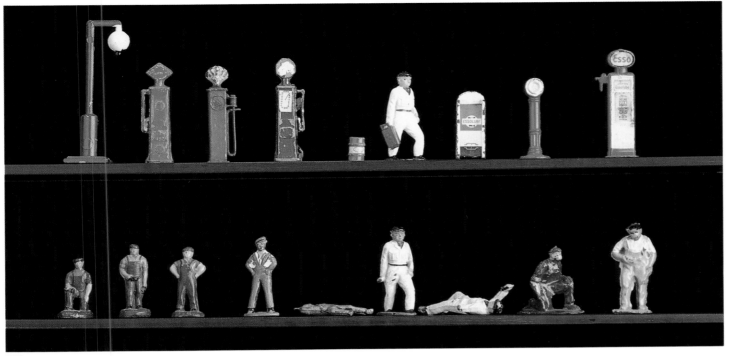

The range of garage figures and accessories issued between 1946 and 1955 is varied to say the least. *Top row:* lamp, first three petrol pumps and fire alarm (second from right) were previously manufactured by John Hill and together with the two mechanics at right (second row) and two die-cast cars (not shown) were issued in Eire by the 'breakaway' faction of Timpo. They are thought not to have been available after 1950. The Esso drum, mechanic with petrol can, oil cabinet and Esso pump were issued in 1952. *2nd row:* first five figures (of which the first three are composition) are pre-1950 found in Timpo boxes and were probably bought in from other makers. The lying and walking mechanics in white overalls with 'Lex' on the back are 1952.

512

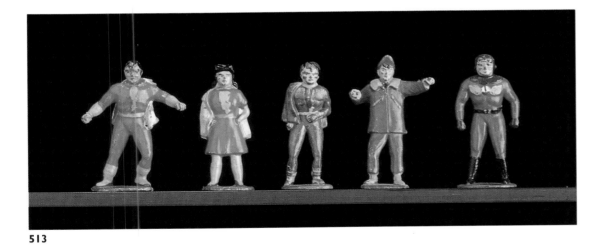

513

514

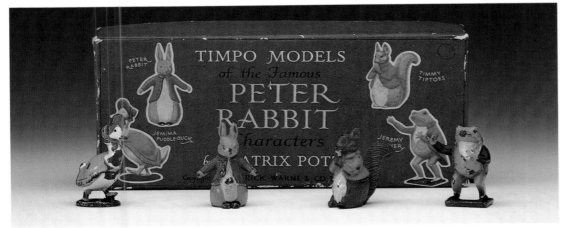

515

513 Super heroes: Captain Marvel, Mary Marvel, Marvel Junior, Icky and Captain Midnight. A very rare set dating to 1954.

514 Tarzan with monkey holding a ball, 1954. Tarzan was issued in small illustrated boxes with a variety of different animals from the Timpo zoo range.

515 Beatrix Potter Peter Rabbit set with Peter, Jeremy Fisher, Timmy Tiptoes and Jemima Puddleduck. This 1954 boxed set is very rare and could sometimes be obtained by purchasing a board game manufactured by Frederick Warne.

This coronation coach in original box issued in 1953 is probably the rarest post-war coronation coach issued. The decorated lamp post is also very rare.

516

The boxed Queen in coronation robes together with the miniature gilt version were issued in 1953. The Queen mounted on 'Winston' was probably a 1954 issue, the version illustrated on the left being sprayed bronze and sold as a souvenir item. The seated Queen is from the inside of the Timpo coronation coach.

517

Rare version of HM the Queen on walking horse, used as part of a window display in a large London department store, 1953. (Courtesy Bill Kingsman)

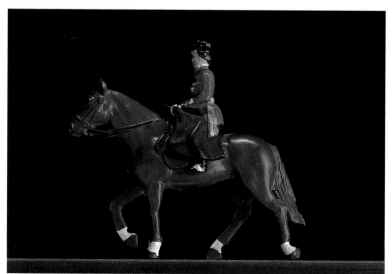

518

548

A range of unidentified military figures, 1893–1966.

Khaki troops and equipment,
1900–46.

549

550, 551
Front and rear views of an Indian
lying over his horse. This splendid
figure is an ingenious design, which
remains unidentified, c.1950.

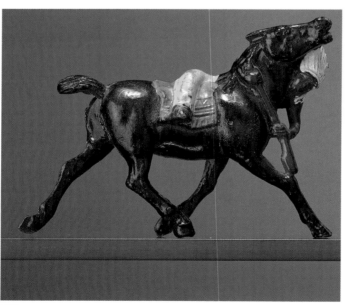

550

551

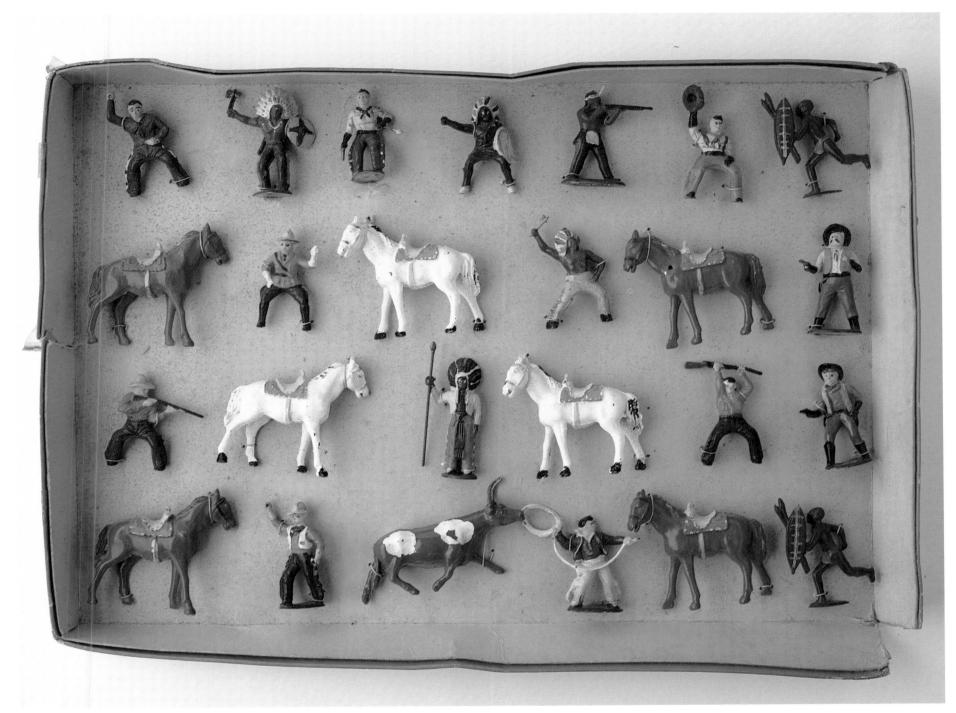

552

Although all the figures contained within this box can be attributed to
Timpo, Harvey, or Benbros, it is not known how this set was marketed
or under whose name, c.1951.
(Courtesy Helen and Martin Fahie)

Cowboys and Indians. The cowboy on bucking bronco is almost certainly by Crescent as is the Davy Crockett figure in row two. Mainly post-war except the first and last figures in row two and the first three Indians in row four.

page 277

554 A varied selection of unidentified civilian figures.
Top row: first two figures possibly Kew; fourth figure possibly John Hill.
2nd row: second and fourth figures possibly Kew or Pixyland; third figure possibly John Hill; last figure possibly Cherilea.
3rd row: third, ninth, tenth, and eleventh figures possibly Kew or Pixyland.
4th row: sixth and seventh made in Japan.

All items pre-war except the first, sixth and tenth figures in row two.

553

554

571

All the street furniture in this illustration has still to be identified. The double lamp standard is possibly an early Taylor & Barrett product. The oil dispenser second row, first left is marked 'M.D'. The 'Pratts' petrol pump has also been found painted silver and is possibly by Kew. The telephone box has a perspex interior giving a glass window effect, while the fire point utilises a cardboard back to support the sandpit and buckets. The hollow-cast gravestone salt and peppers are similar in style to the milestones pictured in the John Hill section.

572 Felix the Cat porcelain head with movable glass eyes, an aluminium Felix and a 70mm hollow-cast version.

573 Station truck in die-cast with its original box.

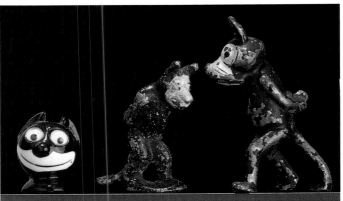

572

573

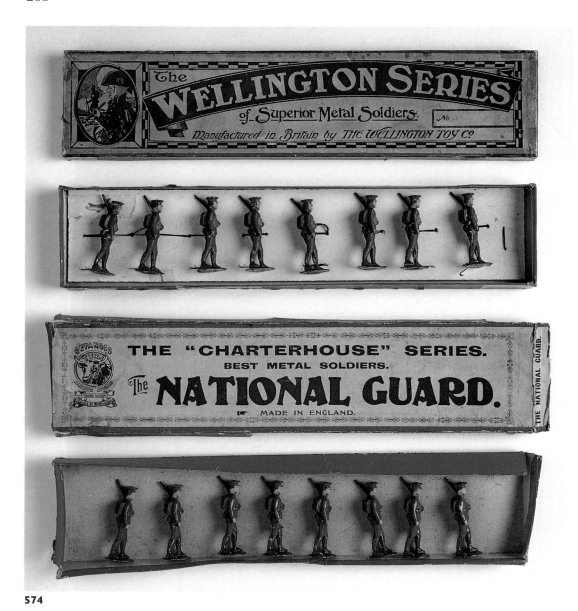

574

WELLINGTON TOY COMPANY

Liverpool, 1916

Marked 'W T C', with oval bases, these soldiers were also issued by Oliver Harper (O H and Company) as part of their 'Unity Series' of guns. B & T utilised some of the moulds during the 1950s. All known examples of the firm's range which consisted of twelve sets are illustrated.

WEND-AL

Dorset, 1948

Although the products of the Wendan Manufacturing Company (better known as Wend-al) were not produced using the hollow-cast method of production, they were sold alongside lead figures in the vast majority of toy shops during the 1950s.

During the late 1940s Mr Edgar Keyhoe conceived the idea of producing aluminium toy figures in England, following an introduction to the owner of the French firm Quiralu. These figures were to be produced from French-made casting plates and were to be advertised as 'unbreakable'. The company, operating from Blandford, Dorset, was known as Wendan, this name being derived from the Christian names of the works manager's daughters Wendy and Ann. 'Wend-al', as the figures became known, was the trade name used for the toy-producing operations as Wendan also manufactured other products. Apart from a few items supplied to Barkers of Kensington in 1960, the last Wend-al figures were released in 1956. Wend-al, together with most hollow-cast manufacturers, could not compete with the introduction of plastic figures. I am very grateful to Giles

575

Brown of Dorset Models whose original research has shed much light on information about Wend-al products.

Identification of Wend-al figures can be easy if the paper label is still attached to the underside of the base. The list of Wend-al products in the inventory at the back is taken from a 1952 price list plus descriptions of figures produced after the issue of that list. It should be assumed that items without catalogue numbers were added to the range between 1952 and 1956.

Some of Wend-al's earlier animal figures were issued with bases, a practice which was discontinued as raw material became more expensive. Wend-al also indulged in the flock-coating process and, along with guardsmen's busbies, many animals were given this treatment. Boxed sets with a drop-down front flap were introduced to display various products. This can be seen to good effect in the case of horse-drawn vehicles.

Several Wend-al items resemble Timpo figures and it is possible that there was a connection between the two companies during 1955, when Timpo were phasing out their hollow-cast range.

576

page 288

574 Two boxes of figures marked WTC for the Wellington Toy Co. The Charterhouse Series box contains figures 'bought in' and packaged by C E Turnbull & Co. (Courtesy James Opie)

575 Known as WTC, it is possible that this series of figures was marketed by Oliver Harper under their 'Unity Series' brand name. Lowland Regiment, Worcestershire Regiment, line infantry in blue and red, Cameronians, Highlander and officer, Waterloo infantry (later reproduced in the 1950s by B & T). Khaki peak cap and officer and medical officer.

577

578

576 Farm advertising poster. (Courtesy Giles Brown)

577 A typical Wend-al box is at the top, the others are advertising posters using the Wend-al name on famous water-colour pictures. (Courtesy Giles Brown)

578 A copy of the Wend-al 1952 price list.

Top row: rubber-tyred horse-drawn rake, tumbril cart.
(Courtesy Sue and Ian Toon)
2nd row: horse-drawn harrow and man.
3rd row: the five items in this row may be former Quiralu items – farmer, farm labourer, cart horse, milkmaid and woman feeding poultry.
4th row: German-style farmer, rare two-wheeled cart and man, land girl and farmer's wife holding hen.
All items c.1948.

579

580

Top row: fully-rounded tree (at left) and flat tree (at right). The five cattle had counterparts painted in different shades. The calf has a base as did all early Wend-al animals. These were removed later to cut costs.
2nd row: horse, foal, cart horse, dog, feeding sheep, sheep, ram and pig.

3rd row: two versions of the feeding goat (the first with base), nanny goat, two sizes of turkey, cockerel, chick, pecking hen, scarce seagull and cat seated on yellow mat.
4th row: fence, man guiding horse-drawn plough, flat bush.
All c.1948.

592

These figures have been described as either Salvation Army, circus or military bandsmen.

Top row: bass drum, side drum, standard bearer, cornet and saxaphone.

2nd row: rare standing side drummer with drum stand, conductor or preacher depending upon which set it was issued in, standing cornet and bass drum player.

3rd row: two sizes of tuba, man with baton and trombone player. All 1948.

593

594

595

594 Two rare Muffin the Mule items, the larger example with hinged leg, 1948.

595 Two of the very rare Three Bears, c.1948.
(Courtesy Sue and Ian Toon)

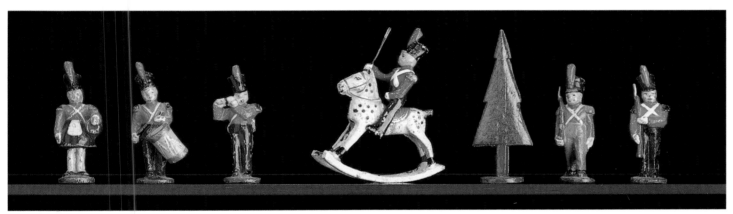

596

Toy Town Series issued in a special box with drop-down front flap enabling the items to be displayed without removing them from the box. Cantinère, drummer, fifer, officers on rocking horse, tree, officer with sword and port arms soldier.

597

Rare Toy Town soldier on rocking horse, c.1948.

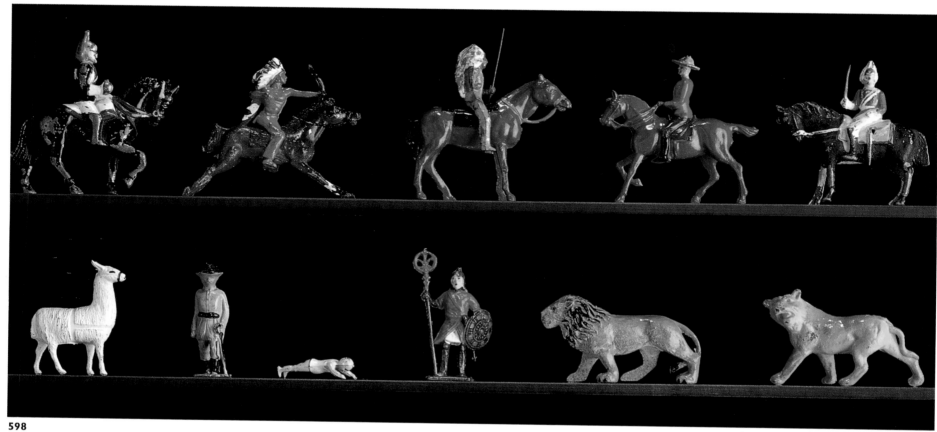

598

One of the most difficult decisions that I faced when compiling this book was when to stop. After many attempts to add new figures I finally called a halt on 16 December 1991. All of the items in this illustration were obtained in the days leading up to the final date for photography. Several more have since turned up. The moral is that a collection of hollow-cast figures will never be complete and this has given me the stimulus to continue with this fascinating hobby.

Top row: MSR Horse Guard, Cherilea Indian chief mounted firing bow and arrow, Charbens Indian chief with spear in movable arm, Crescent pre-war Royal Canadian mounted police and a Charbens mounted Life Guard officer.
2nd row: F G Taylor and Sons llama, John Hill Confederate Officer in campaign hat, Stoddart crawling baby, Cherilea Saracen with standard, F G Taylor and Sons lion and a Cherilea lioness.

INVENTORY OF MANUFACTURERS' PRODUCTS

Catalogue numbers, where known, are listed before the item and are the numbers allocated by the manufacturer. As with the main text, the terms pre- and post-war refer to World War II. If items are listed as pre- and post-war, the pre-war catalogue number is on the left. Some items may acquire different catalogue numbers if they were re-catalogued post-war. Where certain manufacturers' products are not listed, it should be assumed that the full range of that particular firm appears in the A–Z section.

The bold numbers listed after each figure refer to the illustration in which the figure appears within the A–Z section. Two numbers indicate that the item appears in two different illustrations. The bracketed letters (A–E) indicate the rarity of each figure, with (A) unique, (B) very rare, (C) rare, (D) fairly common, (E) very common.

ABEL

Fusilier at slope, movable arms (D)
Guard at slope, movable arm (D)
Highlander at slope (C)
Infantry of line at slope, movable arms (D) **17**
Infantry of line at attention (C)
Mounted British Camel Corps (45mm) (D) **253**
Japanese infantry running at double at trail and shoulder arms (B)
Mounted British line infantry officer (40mm) (B)
Fusiliers and line infantry at the slope were also issued with brass socket at the front of the base in order for them to be used in the Drill Display Frame (C) **16**

The mounted British Camel Corps figure is illustrated in the section devoted to Hanks.

ARGOSY

Muffin the Mule (C) **22**
Peregrin the Penguin (C) **22**
Louise the Lamb (C) **22**
Peter the Dog (C) **22**

ASTRA

1   Lighthouse (Small) (C)
2   Floodlight aerodrome (B)
3   Signal (D)
4   Petrol pump (C)
5   AA gun (D)
6   Searchlight (large) (D)
7   Six-way traffic signal (D)
8   Lightouse (large) (C)
9   Searchlight (small) (D)
10 Searchlight (special) (D)
11 12" Howitzer **23** (D)

1¼" diameter searchlight (D)

3.7 AA gun (D)
Garrison 'fort gun' (D)
Petrol station (C)
Harbour and lighthouse (C)

AVH FARM TOYS

Kayron
504   Horse and rake (E) **557, 558**
513   Horse and milk cart (B)
511   Horse and hay cart (D)

AVH Farm Toys
502   Horse and seed sower (D)

BMC

1   1st Life Guards (D)
2   2nd Life Guards (C) **24**
3   Royal Horse Guards (The Blues) (D) **24**
4   1st (Kings) Dragon Guards (C)
5   2nd Dragoon Guards (Queen's Bays) (C)
6   3rd (Prince of Wales') Dragoon Guards (C)
7   4th (Royal Irish) Dragoon Guards (C)
8   5th (Princess Charlotte of Wales') Dragoon Guards (C)
9   6th Dragoon Guards (Carabiniers) (C)
10   7th (Princess Royal's) Dragoon Guards (C)
11   1st (Royal) Dragoons (C)
12   2nd Dragoons (Royal Scots Greys) (C) **24**
13   3rd (King's Own) Hussars (C)
14   4th (Queen's Own) Hussars (C)
15   5th (Royal Irish) Lancers (C)
16   6th (Inniskilling) Dragoon Guards (C)
17   7th (Queen's Own) Hussars (C)
18   8th (King's Royal Irish) Hussars (C)
19   9th (Queen's Royal) Lancers (C)
20   10th (Prince of Wales' Own Royal) Hussars (C)
21   11th (Prince Albert's Own) Hussars (C)
22   12th (Prince of Wales' Royal) Lancers (C)
23   13th Hussars (C)
24   14th (King's) Hussars (C)

25   15th (The King's) Hussars (C)
26   16th (The Queen's) Lancers (C)
27   17th (Duke of Cambridge's Own) Lancers (C)
28   18th (Queen Mary's Own) Hussars (C)
29   19th (Queen Alexandra's Own Royal) Hussars (C)
30   20th Hussars (C)
31   21st (Empress of India's) Lancers (B)
     Khaki mounted officer (C) **28**

Infantry
32   Grenadier Guards (D)
33   Coldstream Guards (D)
34   Scots Guards (D)
35   Irish Guards (C)
36   The Royal Scots (Lothian Regiment) – 1st Foot (C) **28**
37   The Queen's (Royal West Surrey Regiment) – 2nd Foot (C) **28**
38   The Buffs (East Kent Regiment) – 3rd Foot (D) **28**
39   The King's Own (Royal Lancaster Regiment) – 4th Foot (C)
40   The Northumberland Fusiliers – 5th Foot (C) **28**
41   The Royal Warwickshire Regiment – 6th Foot (C)
42   The Royal Fusiliers (City of London) Regiment – 7th Foot (C)
43   The King's (Liverpool Regiment) – 8th Foot (C)
44   The Norfolk Regiment – 9th Foot (C)
45   The Lincolnshire Regiment – 10th Foot (C)
46   The Devonshire Regiment – 11th Foot (C)
47   The Suffolk Regiment – 12th Foot (C)
48   Prince Albert's (Somerset Light Infantry) – 13th Foot (C)
49   The Prince of Wales Own (West Yorkshire Regiment) – 14th Foot (C)
50   The East Yorkshire Regiment – 15th Foot (C)
51   The Bedfordshire Regiment – 16th Foot (C)
52   The Leicestershire Regiment – 17th Foot (C)
53   The Royal Irish Regiment – 18th Foot (C)
54   Alexandra, Princess of Wales' Own (Yorkshire Regiment) – 19th Foot (C)
55   The Lancashire Fusiliers – 20th Foot (C)
56   The Royal Scots Fusiliers – 21st Foot (C)
57   The Cheshire Regiment – 22nd Foot (C)
58   The Royal Welsh Fusliers – 23rd Foot (C)
59   The South Wales Borderers – 24th Foot (C)

60   The King's Own Scottish Borderers – 25th Foot (C)

61   The Cameronians (Scottish Rifles) 26th and 90th Foot (C)

62   The Royal Inniskilling Fusiliers – 27th and 108th Foot (C)

63   The Gloucestershire Regiment – 28th and 61st Foot (C)

64   The Worcestershire Regiment – 29th and 36th Foot (C)

65   The East Lancashire Regiment – 30th and 59th Foot (C)

66   The East Surrey Regiment – 31st and 70th Foot (C)

67   The Duke of Cornwall's Light Infantry – 32nd and 46th Foot (C)

68   The Duke of Wellings (West Riding Regiment) – 33rd and 76th Foot (C)

69   The Border Regiment – 34th and 55th Foot (C)

70   The Royal Sussex Regiment – 35th and 107th Foot (C)

71   The Hampshire Regiment – 37th and 67th Foot (C)

72   The South Staffordshire Regiment – 38th and 80th Foot (C)

73   The Dorsetshire Regiment – 29th and 54th Foot (C)

74   The Prince of Wales' Volunteers (South Lancashire Regiment) 40th and 82nd Foot (C)

75   The Welsh Regiment – 41st and 69th Foot (C)

76   The Black Watch (Royal Highlanders) – 42nd and 73rd Foot (C) **28**

77   The Oxfordshire and Buckinghamshire Light Infantry – 43rd and 56th Foot (C)

78   The Essex Regiment – 44th and 56th Foot (C)

79   The Sherwood Foresters (Nottinghamshire and Derbyshire Regiment) – 45th and 95th Foot (C)

80   The Loyal North Lancashire Regiment – 47th and 81st Foot (C)

81   The Northamptonshire Regiment – 48th and 58th Foot (C)

82   Princess Charlotte of Wales' (Royal Berkshire Regiment) – 49th and 66th Foot (C)

83   The Queen's Own (Royal West Kent Regiment) – 50th and 97th Foot (C)

84   The King's Own (Yorkshire Light Infantry) – 51st and 105th Foot (C)

85   The King's (Shropshire Light Infantry) – 53rd and 85th Foot (C)

86   The Duke of Cambridge's Own (Middlesex Regiment) – 57th and 77th Foot (C)

87   The King's Royal Rifle Corps – 60th Foot (D)

88   The Duke of Edinburgh's (Wiltshire Regiment) – 62nd and 99th Foot (C)

89   The Manchester Regiment – 63rd and 96th Foot (C)

90   Prince of Wales (North Staffordshire Regiment) – 64th and 98th Foot (C)

91   The York and Lancaster Regiment – 65th and 84th Foot (C)

92   The Durham Light Infantry – 66th and 106th Foot (C)

93   The Highland Light Infantry –71st and 74th Foot (C)

94   Seaforth Highlanders (Ross-shire Buffs, The Duke of Albany's) – 72nd and 78th Foot (C)

95   The Gordon Highlanders – 75th and 92nd Foot (C)

96   The Queen's Own Cameron Highlanders 79th Foot (C)

97   The Royal Irish Rifles – 83rd and 86th Foot (C)

98   Princess Victoria's (Royal Irish Fusiliers) – 87th and 89th Foot (C)

99   The Connaught Rangers – 88th and 94th Foot (C)

100 Princess Louise's (Argyll and Sutherland Highlanders) – 91st and 93rd Foot (C)

101 The Prince of Wales' Leinster Regiment (Royal Canadians) – 100th and 109th Foot (C)

102 The Royal Munster Fusiliers – 101st and 104th Foot (C)

103 The Royal Dublin Fusiliers – 102nd and 103rd Foot (C)

104 The Rifle Brigade (The Prince Consort's Own) (D) **28**

105 London Scottish (D) **28**

106 Pipers of The Scots Guards (C)

107 Pipers of The Argyll and Sutherland Highlanders (C) **28**

The above list of 107 sets come from BMC stock lists and it is possible that not all items were produced.

Foreign Regiments

Austrian infantry (blue) (C) **28**

Russian cavalry (C)

Russian lancers (C)

Austrian infantry (service) (C) **28**

German infantry (blue) (C)

German infantry (service) (C)

French cuirassiers (C) **24**

French infantry (D) **28**

Belgian infantry (D) **28**

Russian cavalry (cossacks) (C) **24**

Russian infantry (C) **28**

Italian bersaglieri (C) **28**

Indians and cowboys, mounted and on foot (E) **24, 27, 28**

Zulus (C) **28**

Boy Scouts (C) **28**

American Boy Scouts (B) **28**

Girl Guides (B)

Firemen (C) **28**

Khaki troop with bicycle (B) **24**

Senior Naval Officer (B) **24**

Royal Navy at Slope (D) **28**

World War I khaki infantry at slope smoking (C) **28**

Khaki infantry, fixed bayonet (C) **28**

Khaki infantry standing firing (D) **28**

Khaki infantry at slope (D) **28**

Line infantry various positions (D) **28**

BENBROS

Figures marked (T) are identical to Timpo figures
The knight marked (C) was also issued by Cherilea

HM Queen Elizabeth mounted on Winston (individual box) (D) **33**

Hussar mounted on prancing horse (D) **37**

Hussar bugler mounted on prancing horse (D) **37**

Dragoon mounted on prancing horse (D) **37**

Dragoon bugler mounted on prancing horse (D) **37**

Dragoon with lance mounted on prancing horse (D) **37**

Life Guard mounted on walking horse (C) **37**

Life Guard on foot (D) **37**

Life Guard on foot with drawn sword (D) **37**

Lancer on foot (D) **37**

Lancer officer on foot with sword in movable arm (C) **37**

Highland piper (B)

Guardsman present arms (C) **37**

Guardsman at slope attention (C) **37**

Guards Band drum major (D) **37**

Guards Band bass drum (D) **37**

Guards Band side drum (D) **37**

Guards Band cymbals (D) **37**

Guards Band sousaphone (D) **37**

Guards Band fife (D) **37**

Guards Band trumpet (D) **37**

Guards Band tuba (D) **37**

Royal Canadian Mounted Police, detachable from horse (D) **39**

Royal Canadian Mounted Police on foot, hands on hips (C) **39**

Knight in silver armour with sword (C) **39**

Robin Hood (C) **38, 39**

Maid Marion (C) **38, 39**

Friar Tuck (C) **38, 39**

Bishop of Hereford (C) **38, 39**

Little John (C) **38, 39**

Will Scarlet (C) **38, 39**

Mutch the Miller's Son (E) **38, 39**

Sheriff of Nottingham (C) **38, 39**

Man at arms (C) **38, 39**

Hind (deer) (C) **38, 39**

Mounted Indian with tomahawk, detachable from horse (D) **41**

Mounted cowboy bandit with two pistols, detachable from horse (D) **41**

Mounted cowboy bandit with one pistol, detachable from horse (D) **41**

Mounted cowboy hat in air, detachable from horse (D) **41**

Mounted Buffalo Bill with lasso, detachable from horse (C) **41**

Mounted cowboy, rifle across waist, detachable from horse (D) **41**

Mounted cowboy with lasso, detachable from horse (D) **41** (T)

Note: Cowboy and Indian models came supplied on two types of horse, one a standing horse with head turned, the other a walking horse. Charbens' horses are almost identical.

Cowboy tied to tree (C) **41**

Cowboy with lasso (D) **41**

Bandit with mask (D) **41** (T)

Cowboy surrending with mask (D) **41**

Crouching cowboy bandit with mail bag (D) **41**

Cowboy with pistol (D) **41**

Sheriff walking with pistol, moustache (C) **41**

Cowboy standing with pistol, moustache (D) **41**

Cowboy clubbing with rifle (D) **41**

Cowboy with pistol, wounded by arrow (D) **41**

Indian brave firing bow and arrow (E) **41** (T)

Indian chief lying hand to forehead (E) **41** (T)

Indian arms raised – rain dance (C) **41**

Zulu (B) **39**

Postman (B) **34**

Farmer (C) **34**

Drover or man to lead shire-horse (E) **35**

Seated girl riding shire-horse (B) **35**

Man with pitchfork and hay (E) **34**

Shire-horse (B) **35**

Cow with bell (C) **34**

Cow feeding (E) **34**

Cow lying (E) **34**

Bull (D) **34**

Calf lying (E) **34**

Calf walking (E) **34**

Donkey (D) **34**

Goat (D) **34**
Pig (D) **34**
Angry gander (E) **34**
Sheep (E) **34**
Cockerel (E) **34**
Covered wagon, four horses and cowboy (D)
Roman chariot (D) **39**
Horse-drawn log wagon (D) **36**
Horse-drawn tumbril cart (C)
Horse-drawn coronation coach (miniature) (D) **33**
Santa Claus, sleigh and four reindeer (miniature) (C) **40**
Coronation coach (E) **33**
State Laundau (miniature) (C)
Cinderella coach (B) **40**
Tree (C) **38, 39**

B & S

Birdhouse (C) **29**
Sundial (C) **29**
Birdbath with ornamental fish (C) **29**
Wheelbarrow (C)
Lawnmower (C) **29**
Garden swing seat (E)

B & T

A26	Zulu with shield (D)	**31**
A25	Zulu with spear (C)	
B150	Guards Band trumpet (E)	
B151	Guards Band bass trumpet (D)	
B152	Flute (E)	**31**
B153	Large drummer (D)	**31**
B154	Small drummer (D)	**31**
B155	Bugler (E)	**31**
B156	Trombone (D)	
C200	Cowboy with rifle (D)	**31**
C202	Cowboy with rifle (D)	
C203	Indian chief (D)	
C204	Indian with bow (D)	**31**
C203	Cowboy with revolvers (D)	**31**
C206	Indian with hatchet (D)	**31**
C207	Indian chief with bow (D)	**31**
C208	Crawling Indian (D)	
C209	Cowboy with raised arm (D)	**31**
H105	Mounted cavalry (D)	
H106	Mounted Grenadier Guard (D)	**31**
SH108	Mounted soldier (D)	
SH112	Life Guard (D)	**30**
S50	Wellington (D)	**31**
S51	Charging grenadier (D)	**31**
S52	Salute (D)	**31**
S53	Royal West (C)	
S56	Marching grenadier (D)	**31**
S59	Scottish, slope arms (D)	**31**
S61	Scottish kneeling (D)	
S62	Australian (C)	**31**
S64	Scottish lying (D)	**31**
S65	Sailor with rifle (D)	**31**
S71	Sailor, slope arms (D)	**31**

S73	Sailor marching (D)	**31**
S63	Royal West charging (D)	
S302	Soldier with bayonet (D)	**31**
S301	Large Scot marching (D)	
	Mounted cowboy on rearing horse (C)	**31**
	Mounted Indian on rearing horse (C)	**31**
	Camel Corps (E)	**31**
	White hunter firing rifle (C)	**31**
	White hunter on elephant (C)	**31**

BRITAINS

Britains' Farm Series

501	Farmer (E)	**47**
502	Farmer's wife (E)	**47**
503	Farmer's wife with umbrella (E)	**47**
504	Carter plain arm (E)	**47**
505	Carter with whip (E)	**47**
506	Horse (shire) (E)	**48**
507	Colt (shire) (E)	**48**
508	Cow (assorted colours) (E)	**48**
509	Calf (assorted colours) (E)	**48**
510	Sheep, walking (E)	**48**
511	Sheep, feeding (E)	**48**
512	Lamb (E)	**48**
513	Dog (E)	**48**
514	Pig (E)	**48**
515	Turkey (E)	**48**
516	Fowl, cock and hen (speckled) (E)	
517	Fowl, cock and hen (white) (E)	
518	Fowl, cock and hen (yellow) (E)	
519	Angry gander (E)	**48**
520	Geese (E)	**48**
521	Oak tree (D)	**50**
522	Cedar tree (D)	**50**
523	Elm tree (D)	**50**
524	Fir tree (D)	**50**
525	Fallen tree (D)	**50**
526	Shrub (D)	**50**
527	Hurdle (E)	**50**
528	Large trough (E)	**50**
529	Small trough (E)	**50**
530	Sheep, lying (E)	**48**
531	Milkmaid with pail on head (D)	**47**
532	Milkmaid carrying pail (E)	**47**
533	Duck (E)	**48**
534	Calf, lying (E)	**48**
535	Landgirl (D)	**47**
536	Sheep and lamb (E)	**48**
537	Milkmaid milking, with pail (E)	**47**
538	Cow, lying (E)	**48**
539	Cow, feeding (E)	**48**
540	Goat (E)	**48**
541	Cart horse (E)	**48**
542	Wheat sheaf, stacked (E)	**50**
543	Horse, feeding (E)	**48**
544	Chicks (assorted positions) (D)	**48**
545	Sitting hen (E)	**48**
546	Piglets (Assorted colours and sizes) (E)	**48**
547	Man with wheelbarrow (D)	**47**
548	Hedge and field gate (D)	**50**

549	Hedge and garden gate (D)	**50**
550	Cob (E)	**48**
551	Scarecrow (D)	**47**
552	Donkey (E)	**48**
553	Sheaf of wheat, single (D)	**50**
554	Farmer's son, sitting (D)	**47**
555	Aged villager, man, sitting (E)	**47**
556	Aged villager, woman, sitting (E)	**47**
557	Village girl, walking (C)	**47**
558	Village boy, walking with stick (C)	**47**
559	Young lady walking (C)	**47**
560	Farm hand, sitting, for driving farm machine (D)	**47**
561	Farmer's daughter, sitting (D)	**47**
562	Golfer, walking (C)	**47, 99**
563	Stable lad, walking (E)	**47**
564	Man with swing water barrow (D)	**47**
565	Goslings (assorted positions) (D)	**48**
566	Field hayrack (E)	**50**
567	Log seat (E)	**50**
568	Garden seat (D)	**50**
569	Dog kennel (D)	**50**
570	Dog kennel with baseboard (C)	**50**
571	Dog for kennel, lying (D)	**48, 50**
572	Dog for kennel, sitting (D)	**48, 50**
573	Bull (E)	**48**
574	Telegraph pole (C)	**50**
575	Dovecote (E)	**50**
576	Dog, St Bernard (D)	**48**
577	Shepherd, with crook (D)	**47**
578	AA Scouts (assorted) (C)	**47, 94**
579	AA sign (destination) Crawley (C)	**94**
580	AA sign (caution) 'School' sign (C)	**50**
581	Rustic stile (D)	**50**
582	Signpost (one direction) (D)	**50**
583	Signpost (two directions) (D)	
584	Signpost (three directions) (D)	**50**
586	Fencing (E)	**50**
587	Village idiot (C)	**47**
588	Milk churn (D)	**50**
589	Blacksmith with anvil (D)	**47**
590	Pail (D)	**50**
591	Dairyman with yoke and pails (D)	**47**
592	Curate (C)	**47**
593	Country clergyman (D)	**47**
594	Shepherd with lamb (D)	**47**
595	Shepherd boy with lantern (C)	**47**
596	Berkshire pigs (boars and sows) (D)	**48**
597	Exmoor Horn sheep (ewe and ram in full fleece) (D)	**49**
598	Gentleman farmer, mounted (D)	**47**
599	Jersey cow (champion) (D)	**49**
600	Boy on Shetland pony (D)	**47**
601	Hampshire Down ram (D)	**49**
602	Foal (E)	**49**
603	Rabbit (D)	**49**
604	Cat (D)	**49**
605	Greyhound, standing (C)	**49**
606	Greyhound, running (C)	**49**
607	Girl Guide and Guider (B/C)	**47, 80**
608	Huntsman, mounted (D)	**54**
609	Huntswoman, mounted (D)	**54**
610	Huntsman, mounted, galloping (D)	**54**

611 Huntswoman, mounted, galloping (D) **54**
612 Huntsman, standing (E) **54**
613 Huntswoman, standing (E) **54**
614 Hounds, standing (assorted positions) (D) **54**
615 Hound, running (D) **54**
616 Fox (D) **54**
617 Table (C) **50**
618 See-saw, with boy and girl (C) **50**
619 Garden swing, with boy (C) **50**
620 Hare, running (D) **49**
621 Traffic policeman (E) **47**
622 Swan and five cygnets (C) **49**
623 Huntswoman, mounted, astride (C) **47, 54**
624-634 Flint wall
624 Straight section (C) **68**
625 Round corner section (C)
626 Stile (C) **68**
627 Gate post section (C) **68**
628 Short cross section (C) **68**
629 Square corner section (C) **68**
630 Five barred gate (large) (C) **68**
631 Five barred gate (small) (C)
632 Tryst gate frame (C)
633 Stone pier (C) **68**
634 Stone pier for gate (C) **68**
635 Tinplate pond (B) **51**
636 Rabbit, sitting up (C) **49**
637 Dog, begging (C) **49**
638 Spiteful cat (C) **49**
639 Shrubs (assorted) (C) **50**
640 Tree (D) **50**
641 Motor cycle with sidecar (B)
642 Rhode Island Red (prize poultry), assorted cocks and hens (B)
643 White Leghorn (prize poultry), assorted cocks and hens (B) **49**
644 Black Plymouth Rock (prize poultry), assorted cocks and hens, correctly coloured to represent the different breeds (B)
645 Navvy with pickaxe (C) **47**
646 Navvy with shovel (C) **47**
647 Highland cattle (D) **49**
648 Field horse (E) **49**
649 Field horse (E) **49**
650 Blacksmith (D) **47**
651 Anvil (E) **47**
652 Milk roundsman (C) **47**
653 Man on motor cycle (B)
659 Policeman, peak cap (C) **47**
660 Prize poultry, assorted cocks and hens, feeding (C)
666-667 Part of the Garden Series
666 Stone pier for stone walling (C) **68**
667 Garden roller (D)
668 Crazy paving (D) **68**
669 Sundial (D) **68**
670 Wheelbarrow (D)
671 Stone walling (D) **68**
672 Fencing (C)
673 Lawn mower (C)
674 Stone balustrading (C) **68**
675 Cold frame (C) **68**

676 Hose reel (C)
677 Pond (C)
678 Man for wheelbarrow (E)
679 Man for mower (B) **68**
680 Man for roller (C)

The following are pre-war only issues – no catalogue numbers:
Young horse dated 15.8.1903 (B) **46**
US Girl Scout (B) **46, 81**
US policeman, peak cap, directing traffic (B) **46**
RAC man (B) **78**

Farm oddities
It is not known if the following items were produced pre- or post-war as they were not allocated specific catalogue numbers:
Jersey cow with bell (B) **46**
Farmer's wife – fixed arm (A) **46**
Walking donkey (C) **46**
Orange-dipped sheep (C) **46**

Post-war issues
The following were new designs, or reissued items with a new catalogue number:

573 Bull (D) **49**
715 Man with garden roller (see 667 and 680 in pre-war list) (D) **49**
744 Man sowing seed (C) **49**
745 Woman's land army (D) **49**
746 Berkshire sow with litter of piglets (C) **49**
747 Girl with feeding bucket (C) **49**
756 Wild horse (also included in Wild West Set) (D) **49**
758 Bullock (also included in Wild West set) (D) **49**
769 Field horse (replaced 648 and 649 in pre-war listings) (E) **49**
775 Mounted policeman (issued only in boxed sets pre-war) (E) **49**
776 Policeman in helmet (issued pre-war in Railway Set 1R) (C) **76, 78**
779 Painter's ladder (B) **101**
780 Man painting, to stand on 779 (B) **101**
781 Painter to carry ladder (B) **101**
782 Suffolk mare (C) **49**
783 Suffolk foal (C) **49**
784 Ayrshire bull (B) **49**
785 Ayrshire cow (B) **49**
786 Ayrshire calf (B) **49**
787 Garage hand (C) **95**

The following were available in more than one colour variation: 744, 746, 747, 776, 787.

Pre-war summary
The following numbers are items which were produced pre-war only. All others listed up to number 680 were issued both pre- and post-war. 517, 518, 521, 522, 525, 531, 535, 549, 553, 554, 557, 558, 561, 562, 570 (issued as single items post-war), 578, 579, 580, 585 (this number does not appear to have been allocated a product), 587, 592, 617, 624-639, 642, 644, 653, 654-658, 659 (no product allocated), 661-665 (no products allocated), 665, 671-674, 676, 677, 678 and 680 (both issued post-war with their respective equipment), 679.

Colour variations
All except the following are known to have been issued in one or more colour variations: 515, 519, 520, 521, 523, 524, 525, 526, 527, 542, 544, 548, 549, 553, 565, 567, 569, 570, 574, 576, 579, 580, 581, 582, 583, 584, 586, 590, 592, 598, 599, 617, 622, 624-634, 651, 652, 659.

Britains' Hunting Series
608 Huntsman, mounted (D) **54**
609 Huntswoman, mounted, top hat or derby (D) **54**
610 Huntsman, mounted, galloping, top hat or derby (D) **54**
611 Huntswoman, mounted, galloping, top hat or derby (D) **54**
612 Huntsman, standing (E) **54**
613 Huntswoman, standing (E) **54**
614 Hounds, standing (assorted positions) (D) **54**
615 Hound, running (D) **54**
616 Fox (D) **54**
623 Huntswoman, mounted astride (C) **47, 54**

Variations
608 A rare version exists wearing a top hat rather than a jockey type cap (B)
610 A rare jockey cap version also exists (B)
613 Huntswoman standing (B) – American collector Joe Kunzelmann owns a rare red-coated colour variation

Britains' horse-drawn vehicles and accessories
In common with other sections in this book models representing motorised vehicles have not been included.

4F Tumbril cart (E) **55**
5F Farm waggon (E) **55**
6F General purpose plough (E) **55**
7F Tree and gate (C) **56**
8F Horse rake (E) **55**
9F Horse roller (E) **55**
12F Timber carriage, with real log (C) **56**
19F Tree and gate with swing (C) **50**
20F Farmer's gig (C) **56**
30F Fencing with gate specially designed to lock together (B)
40F Farm cart and horse (E) **56**
45F Milk float and horse (D)
58F Fully modelled tree (C) **69**

Post-war only
126F Rubber-tyred horse-drawn farm cart (D) **56**
129F Timber trailer, rubber-tyred (C)
130F Trailer, rubber-tyred (D)
131F Horse-drawn milk float and milkman with 'Britains Dairy' signs (D) **56**
142F Single horse general-purpose plough and ploughman (D) **56**
144F Haystack – papier mâché (B) **53**

Variations
Apart from colour variations, only the following items have more than one structural or content variation:

9F Horse roller: pre-war the roller was in two sections (D) **55**

12F   Timber carriage: the first version contained a fur-hoofed heavy horse pre-war (C) **55**
20F   Farmer's gig: pre-war this item had wire shafts (C) **56** Post-war die-cast shafts

Britains' Zoo Series
901   Indian elephant (C) **62**
902   Grey or red kangaroo (E) **62**
903   Penguin (E) **62**
904   Monkey (E) **62**
905   Hippopotamus or river horse (C) **62**
906   Gorilla (D) **62**
907   Zebra (E) **62**
908   Indian rhinoceros (C) **62**
909   Pelican (E) **62**
910   Lion (E) **62**
911   Lioness (E) **62**
912   Giraffe (B) **61**
913   Pelican (E) **62**
914   Polar bear (E) **62**
915   Chimpanzee (D) **62**
916   King penguin (D) **62**
917   Nile crocodile (C) **62**
918   Bactrian camel (D) **62**
919   Coconut palm (C) **61**
920   Date palm (C) **61**
921   Guenon monkey (walking) (E) **62**
922   Ostrich (E) **62**
923   Llama (E) **62**
924   Gate with posts (C) **61**
925   Railings, straight section (D)
926   Railings, curved section (D)
927   Standard post, two way (straight) (C)
928   Standard post, two way (right angle) (C)
929   Standard post, three way (C)
930   Standard post, four way (C)
931   Keepers (D) **61**
932   Keeper seated astride (B) **61**
933   Eland bull (D) **62**
934   Brown bear (E) **62**
935   American bison (D) **62**
936   Cub bears (E) **62**
937   Giant tortoise (D) **63**
938   Howdah for elephant (B) **61**
939   Boy or girl for howdah (B) **61**
940   Baby hippopotamus (E) **63**
941   Tiger (E) **63**
942   Wild boar (E) **63**
943   Baby camel (E) **63**
944   Baby elephant (D) **63**
945   Sable antelope (D) **63**
946   Stork (E) **63**
947   Flamingo (E) **63**
948   Wart-hog (E) **63**
949   Malay tapir (E) **63**
950   Baby kangaroo or wallaby (E) **63**
951   Baby rhinoceros (D) **63**
952   Young Indian elephant (D) **63**
953   Bactrian camel with boy rider (B) **61**
954   Gorilla with pole (D) **63**
955   Wolf (D) **63**

956   Walrus (D) **63**
957   Red deer (C) **63**
958   Young crocodile (D) **63**
959   Young hippopotamus (D) **63**
960   Young rhinoceros (D) **63**
961   Young giraffe (D) **61**
962   Lion cub (sitting) (D) **63**
963   Gazelle (C) **63**
964   Sea lion (E) **63**
965   Himalayan bear (sitting) (E) **63**
966   Polar bear (walking) (E) **63**
967   Polar bear (standing) (E) **63**
968   Indian or water buffalo (D) **63**
969   Giant panda (D) **63**
970   Baby panda (assorted positions) (D) **63**
971   The panda family (containing giant panda and two baby pandas) (B)

In 1991 a wildebeest (A) was discovered and is thought to have been destined for issue just prior to the suspension of production before World War II. No catalogue descriptions exist for 972-975. The first post-war number was 976. Keepers listed under 931 came in two sizes. A rare keeper in green was discovered in 1992 (A).

Pre-war summary
The following were issued pre-war only, all others up to number 969 were issued both pre- and post-war:

901   Elephant with rubber trunk (B)
912   Adult giraffe (B) **61**
932   Keeper seated astride (only issued in boxed set 242 post-war) (B) **61**
938   Howdah for elephant (B) **61**
939   Boy or girl for howdah as 932 (B) **61**
971   Panda family in individual box (B)

Post-war summary
The following were post-war issues:

976   Boy in sailor suite to ride camel (issued also as part of 953) (B) **61**
978   Baby chimpanzee (B) **60**
986   Panther (C) **60**
987   Baboon (C) **60**
988   Springbuck (C) **60**
989   Bushbuck (B) **60**
990   Vulture (C) **60**
991   King cobra (C) **60**
992   Seated tiger (D) **60**
993   Curved sections of railing (C) **61**
994   Straight sections of railing (C) **61**

Britains' Mammoth Circus
351B   Prancing horse (D) **70**
352B   Trotting horse (D) **70**
353B   Man on stilts (D) **70**
354B   Clown with hoop (D) **70**
355B   Equestrienne (D) **70**
356B   Cowboy with lasso (B) **70**
357B   Ring master (D) **70**
358B   Clown, standing (D) **70**
359B   Elephant (D) **70**

446B   Tub (D) **70**
447B   Boxing clown (C) **70**
448B   Lion tamer (D) **70**
449B   Performing tiger (D) **70**
450B   Performing elephant (C) **70**
451B   Boxing kangaroo (C) **70**
1439   Roundabout (B) **72**
1141   The flying trapeze (B) **71**

The cowboy 356B was issued pre-war only. Taken from the Wild West Series, it has a brown base rather than green.

Britains' Miniature Garden
01   Flower bed with grass border (straight section) (D) **66**
02   Flower bed with grass border (finishing circular section) (D) **66**
03   Flower bed with grass border (return square section) (D) **66**
04   Flower bed with grass border (return circular section) (D)
05   Flower bed with grass border (half straight section) (D) **66**
06   Flower bed with grass border (finishing corner section) (D) **66**
07   Post for stone wall (D) **68**
08   Garden roller (D)
09   Crazy paving (D) **68**
10   Sundial on pedestal (D) **68**
11   Garden wheelbarrow (D)
12   Stone wall (D) **68**
13   Pergola section (B)
14   Rustic arch (C) **68**
15   Mound (C) **66**
16   Coloured vase (C) **68**
17   Garden seat (D) **50**
18   Interlaced board fence with trellis (D) **68**
19   Rambler rose (B) **66**
20   Lobelia (C) **66**
21   Geranium (C) **66**
22   Torch lily – red-hot poker (C) **66**
23   Conifer (C) **66**
24   Sunflower (C) **66**
25   Poppy (C) **66**
26   Lupin (C) **66**
27   Half standard rose (C) **66**
28   Bush rose (C)
29   Aster (C) **66**
30   Hollyhock (double) (C) **66**
31   Antirrhinum (C) **66**
32   Dahlia (double) (C) **66**
33   Dahlia (single) (C) **66**
34   Gladioli (C) **66**
35   Wallflower (C)
36   Foxglove (C) **66**
37   Chrysanthemum (C) **66**
38   Full standard rose (C)
39   Delphinium (C) **66**
40   Hyacinth (C) **66**
41   Tulip (C) **66**
42   Crocus (C) **66**
43   Snowdrop (C) **66**
44   Daffodil (C) **66**

Grenade thrower (E) **198**
Flame thrower (E) **198**
Mounted officer (E) **198**

Various items from Crescent's khaki ranges were issued in sand-coloured uniforms just prior to the firm switching to plastic production in the mid-1950s (C).

Guardsmen, Life Guards and Highlanders
Guardsman at ready (E) **171**
Guardsman standing firing (E) **171**
Guardsman lying firing (E) **171**
Guardsman kneeling firing (E) **171**
Guardsman at slope (E) **171**
Guardsman saluting (E) **171**
Guardsman at ease (E) **171**
Life Guard at attention (E) **199**
Mounted guardsman at trot (E) **199**
Mounted Life Guard at trot (E) **199**
Sentry box (E) **171**
Guardsman, movable arm, at slope (E) **171**

Guards Bandsmen
Side drummer (E) **171**
Fife (E) **171**
Trombone (E) **171**
Bugler standing (E) **171**
Bassoon (E) **171**
Tuba (E) **171**
Cymbals (E) **171**
Bugler (E) **171**
Highlander lying firing (E) **171**
Highlander kneeling firing (E) **171**
Highlander at slope (E) **171**
Highland piper (E) **171**
Mounted Scots Grey (D) **199**
State trumpeter (D) **171**
Highlander kneeling, fixed bayonet (D) **171**

RAF
Machine gunner (also issued as khaki) (C) **200**
Kneeling radio operator (also issued as khaki) (C) **200**
Mechanic (also issued as railway personnel) (E) **196**
Man guiding aeroplanes in to land (C) **200**
At slope (also issued in khaki) (C) **200**
Fire fighting (also issued as Dan Dare) (C) **200**
Pilot with documents (D) **200**
Officer saluting (also issued as Digby) (D) **200**
Officer marching (also issued as Dan Dare) (D) **200**
Airman in forage cap and greatcoat (D) **200**
Airman in forage cap, slung rifle (C) **200**

Royal Canadian Mounted Police
Mounted officer, turning in saddle (C) **174**
Kneeling (C) **174**
Kneeling firing pistol (C) **174**
Standing firing rifle (C) **174**
At ease (C) **174**
Standing firing pistol (C) **174**
Marching at slope (E) **174**

USA Marines
At slope (C) **200**

At attention (C) **200**
At ease (C) **200**

Navy
Sailor, white uniform marching (E) **200**
US sailor at slope, white uniform, movable arm (C) **200**
US sailor at slope, blue uniform, movable arm (C) **200**
US sailor, slope, fixed arm (B) **200**

Others
Khaki soldier, steel helmet, rifle slung on back (D)
Fireman with axe (C) **196**
Petrol pump Shell (D) **196**
Petrol pump Esso (D) **196**
Air line (D) **196**
Mounted policeman, removable from horse (D) **196**
Home Guard at attention with stick (D) **172**
Khaki soldier in forage cap, marching empty handed (C) **172**
Artillery officer, hand raised (B) **181**
West Point Cadet, fixed arm, at slope (C) **174**
Seated Arab with rifle (D) **174**

Between 1947 and 1955 Crescent issued the following sets in small colourful boxes.

580 **Cowpunchers Set**
Mounted cowboy, detachable from horse issued with running steer or calf from Rodeo Set (2200) (D) **190**

1100 **Grand-Ma and Grand-Pa Set**
High back settee, Grand-Ma sitting knitting, Grand-Pa with stick, table, dog and cups and saucers (C) **201**

1101 **'Junior Miss' Set**
Dressing table with mirror and fitments, chair and 'Junior Miss' (B) **203**

1216 **Tuglift**
Station platform trucking system with milk churns and packing case (B) **212**

1222 **Builders and Decorators Set**
Hand cart, builder to push, bucket and ladder (B) **212**

1224 **Deep Sea Diver Set**
Diver, removable helmet, safety line, air pump, tie bollards, hatchet and knife. 2 versions (B) **221**

1225 **Our Doggies Set**
Kennel, dog standing, dog eating, 'Beware of Dog' sign, feeding bowls and bones (B) **208**

1226 **Duck Pond Set**
Duck pond, swimming ducks and stork standing on the bank of the pond (B) **217**

1227 **School Days Set**
Male and female teacher, male and female dunce, teacher's desk and blackboard, school desks, seated school children, school crossing warden and matron (B) **205**

1229 **GPO Engineers' Set**
Two telegraph poles, hand truck safety guard and cover, bucket, man to climb pole, man with coil of

wire, kneeling man with head phones, engineer feeding wire (B) **211**

1230 **Butchers Shop Set**
Counter, butcher's bench with meat, butcher with cleaver, butcher's assistant, scales and two female customers (B) **213**

1231 **Fish and Chip Shop Set**
Frying range, counter, assistant, 'Frying Tonight' sign, chips and fish and two female customers (B) **214**

1237 **Ice Cream Parlour Set (Milk Bar)**
Milk bar and counter, high stools, tea urn, fridge, assistant, male and female children customers and ice creams (B) **215**

1246 **Hen Coop Set**
Hen coop, farm girl with bucket and various hens and chickens (C) **193**

1540 **Red Cross Stretcher Party**
Light blue uniforms (D) **175**

1802 **Tractor and Hay Rake Set**
Tractor and female farm hand driver. Trailer with female farmhand passenger (D) **222**

1818 Tumbril cart and horse (D) **218**

1819 Four-wheel horsedrawn farm wagon (D) **218**

2211 **Hospital Set**
Nurse, sister, doctor, beds (with real linen bedclothes), bedside cabinet, children patients, vases of flowers and cups (B) **206**

2701 **Stage Coach Set**
Stagecoach with galloping horses, driver and shotgun (D) **189**

2754 **Medieval Fort Set**
Sectional medieval fort with various knights (D) **185**

Barber's Shop Set
Wash basins, stand and mirrors, barber with razor, barber's chairs and seated customers with robes (B) **216**

Dan Dare Set
Dan Dare walking, Digby saluting, Treen, Professor Peabody, rocket ship and launcher, Dan Dare in space suit (B) **220**

Dial 999 Set (die-cast)
Police car, burglar being attacked by police dog and handler, burglar with loot and policeman with truncheon (B) **223**

Coronation Coach
12½" long coach with footman and beefeater (D) **199**

Garden Tea Party Set
Four chairs, two girls, two boys, table with sun shade, cups saucers and plates (B) **204**

Farmer's Market Wagon Set
Horse-drawn wagon, farmer with pitchfork dog and pigs (C)

Goldilocks and the Three Bears Set
Goldilocks in blue dress holding wide brim hat, Father, Mother and Baby Bear (B) **224, 225**

Garden Tea Party Set
Four chairs, two girls, two boys, table with sun shade, cups saucers and plates (B) **204**

Calling All Cars Set (die-cast)
Police car, policeman directing traffic, burglar throwing brick at jeweller's window (B) **221**

Rabbit Hutch
Rabbit hutch and rabbits lying and sitting (B) **193**

Dodgem Car Set
Dodgem car, sparking rail and child passengers (B) **202**

Spanish bullfighter and bull (B) **226**
Rickshaw with European lady and man, pulled by Zulu (C) **227**
Ostrich-drawn rickshaw (B) **227**
Timber wagon (B) **219**

FRY

Khaki, peak cap, seated machine gunner (E) **242, 244**
Khaki, peak cap, motor cycle and rider (D) **242, 243, 244**
Khaki 'gentleman in khaki' with bandaged head (B) **242, 244**
Canadian advancing with fixed bayonet (D) **242, 244, 245**
Australian advancing with fixed bayonet (D) **242, 244, 245**
Australian at ready (D) **242, 244, 245**
Scottish grenade thrower (D) **244**
Highlander, bayonet down (C) **244**
Highlander, shorten arms (C) **244**
London Scottish, bayonet down (C) **244**
London Scottish, shorten arms (C) **244**
Highlander at slope (D) **244**
Khaki, peak cap at slope (D)
Khaki, peak cap, charging (D) **244**
Rifle brigade, at slope (B)
Red jacketed, peak cap, charging (D) **244**
Khaki, peak cap, standing firing (E) **244**
Khaki, steel helmet advancing with fixed bayonet (E) **244**
Khaki, peak cap, advancing with fixed bayonet (E) **244**
Khaki 'bomb thrower', steel helmet (E) **244**

Khaki, peak cap, port arms (C) **244**
Khaki, peak cap, lying firing (E) **244**
Sailor, blue jacket, advancing with fixed bayonet (D) **244**
Sailor, white jacket, advancing with fixed bayonet (C)
Barbed wire (C) **242, 244**
Cavalry officer with sword (C) **244**
Nurse (C) **244**
Belgian infantry kneeling (C) **244**
Belgian infantry advancing (C) **244**
German surrendering (C) **244**
Bersaglieri advancing with fixed bayonet (C) **244**
French infantry, bayonet down (B) **244**
Australian port arms (C) **244**
Russian charging (B)
'Dough boy' charging (D)
French machine gunner (C) **244**

HANKS

Many of Hanks items were direct copies of Britains. The items listed are those which are not 'pirated' models.

Camel Corps (C) **254**
Lancer (C) **254**
Red Indian chief with Tomahawk, large scale (C) **254**
Peak cap khaki infantry slope, large scale (C) **254**
Infantry of line, large scale (B) **254**
Boy scout with pole, large scale (B) **254**
Guards officer (D) **253, 254**
Guardsman standing firing (E) **253**
Guardsman slope (E) **254**
Guardsman trail (D) **254**
Guards drummer (D) **253, 254**
Infantry of line, trail (D) **254**
Infantry of line at slope (D) **254**
Infantry of line kneeling to receive cavalry (D) **254**
Highlander at slope (D) **254**
Khaki, peak cap, at slope (D) **254**
Khaki, peak cap, lying firing (D) **254**
Khaki, peak cap, kneeling to receive cavalry (D) **254**
Zulu, movable arm (B) **254**

Zulu running with spear (C) **254**
Zulu running with shield and knobkerry (C) **254**
Zulu in loin cloth with shield and spear (C) **254**
Sailor running at trail (C)
Boy Scout at attention with pole, fixed arm (B) **254**
Scoutmaster, movable arm (B) **254**
Scout with pole, movable arm (C) **254**
Scout with two movable arms to push trek cart (B) **254**

H R PRODUCTS

Viking chief with winged helmet (C) **259**
Viking drawing dagger (C) **259**
Viking holding axe (C) **259**
Viking attacking with axe (C) **259**
Viking with dagger (C) **259**
(All available in red, green, light blue or dark blue colours)

Roman centurion (C) **259**
Roman legionnaire (C) **259**
Knight with sword and shield (C) **257**
Knight with lancer (C) **257**
Knight with halberd (C) **257**

Pirates, Fact and Fiction
(available in boxed set or individual boxes)

Long John Silver (C) **258**
Cutty Carver (C) **258**
Wall Eye Jim (C) **258**
Captain Hook (C) **258**
Black Jack (C) **258**

Policemen
Policeman standing hands behind back (C) **259**
Policeman directing traffic (C) **259**
Policeman in white coat directing traffic (C) **259**
Policeman in overcoat directing traffic (C) **259**
Mounted policeman (C) **259**

The Bumblies, one, two and three (B) **260**

J HILL & CO

PRE-WAR ISSUES
(with post-war cross reference)

Ancient John Hill
The following items are thought to have been issued pre-World War I:

Guardsman at slope, movable arm (B) **261, 272**
Indian crawling on all fours with knife and rifle (B) **316**

Pre-	Post-war		
4P		Mounted Life Guard (smaller than standard) (D)	
4		Khaki cavalry (smaller than standard) (D)	**263**
5P		Infantry of line at the ready (D)	**262, 268**
6P	11	Mounted Life Guard (D)	**269**
9A		Khaki infantry, peak cap, charging (E)	**263**
10A		Khaki infantry, peak cap, standing firing (E)	**263**
11A	51	Gordon Highlander, kneeling (also issued in khaki) (D)	**267**
11AC	51	(Second grade paint version of 11A) (E)	
12A	52	Argyle and Sutherland Highlander prone (lying firing), legs apart (E)	**267**
12AC	52	Prone Highlander (lying firing) (second grade version of 12A) (E)	**267**
13B		Khaki bugler, peak cap (also issued in red tunic) (E)	**263**
13D		Khaki drummer, peak cap (E)	**263**
16AP	50	Black Watch, at slope with fixed arm (issued also in khaki and with khaki socks (E/D/C)	**267**
19A	601	Cowboy with rifle at ready (E)	**317**
19C	601	(Second grade paint version of 19A) (E)	
20A	616	Indian brave holding rifle barrel (E)	**317**
20AC	615	Indian on foot, creeping with tomahawk (D)	**317**
20C	618	Indian chief with tomahawk (D)	**317**
20S	615	Indian creeping (second grade paint version of 20AC) (E)	
20T	618	Indian chief, fixed arm with tomahawk (second grade paint version of 20C) (E)	
21A	61	Kneeling sailor (issued in blue and white uniform) (D)	**273**
21C		Second grade paint version of 21A (D)	
26A	608	Mounted cowboy firing revolver, movable arm (D)	**316**
27A		North American Indian, advancing with rifle (E)	**317**

Pre-	Post-war	
27C		(Second grade paint version of 27A) (E)
31A		Mounted khaki lancer (also issued in red tunic), movable arm (C) **263**
33P	15	Mounted Scots Grey (D) **270**
40P	17	Mounted Arab, rifle in air (D) **278**
47A	60	Sailor standing at ready (issued in blue and white uniforms) (D) **273**
47C	60	(Second grade paint version of 47A) (D)
50/1	72	Grenadier Guard, drum major (D) **271, 272**
50/2	73	Grenadier Guard, bass drummer (D) **271, 272**
50/3	80	Grenadier Guard, side drum (D) **271, 272**
50/4	74	Grenadier Guard, saxhorn (D) **271, 272**
50/5	78	Grenadier Guard, trumpet (D) **271, 272**
50/6	79	Grenadier Guard, trombone (D) **271, 272**
50/7	76	Grenadier Guard, clarinet (D) **271, 272**
50/8	71	Grenadier Guard, fife (D) **271, 272**
50/9	75	Grenadier Guard, cymbals (D) **271, 272**
105A		Race horse and jockey (C) **299**
106A		Zulu charging (D) **277**
106C		(Second grade paint version of 106A) (D)
107B		Boy Scout bugler (B)
107C		Boy Scout with pole (B)
107D		Boy Scout drummer (B)
156		Policeman (larger than standard) (C) **290**
171L	41	Knight on foot, movable arm (E) **280**
172L	6	Knight mounted with lance, movable arm (E) **280**
176P		Camel with rider (also issued in gilt) (D) **278**
177P		Elephant with rider (D) **278**
178P	623	Mounted Indian, galloping (D) **316**
191A		Small submarine and large submarine (C)
191C		
213A		Mounted hussar on standing horse (B) **269**
215A	30	Scots Guard at slope, movable arm (E) **272**
215P	549/S	Piper (issued in various tartans, also khaki) (E) **267**
243A	37	Grenadier Guard, running trail, movable arm (D) **272**
244A	32	Black Watch marching, movable arm, at slope (E) **267**
245A		Manchester Regiment, running trail, movable arm (D) **268**
249L	627	Cowboy riding bucking bronco (C) **316**
251L		Cowboy mounted with lasso, movable arm (D) **316**
260P		Mounted cowboy, firing rifle (E) **316**
261P	21	Mounted Arab (D) **278**
265C	617	Crawling Indian (E) **317**
267B		Airship (C) **273**
267MC		RAF mechanic (D) **273**
267PC		RAF pilot (D) **273**
267RC		RAF rigger (D) **273**
303L	606	Cowboy on foot with lasso, movable arm (D) **317**
304L	625	Cowgirl with whip, movable arm (D) **317**
305L	629	Cowboy to ride steer (C) **316**
451C	K69	Khaki officer, peak cap (C) **263**
461		'Bisley' tent and flag (C)
462		'Whitehall' sentry box with mounted Life Guard (C)
463		Sentry box (D)
464		'Tower' sentry box with guardsman (C)
465		'Tower' sentry box (C)
501A		Mounted Indian with rifle (E) **316**
523A		
523C	58	Firing fusilier (E) **268**
524A	55	Lincolnshire Regiment firing (blue helmet) (D) **268**
524C	55	As 524A (D)
530A	602	Cowboy firing revolver (E) **312, 317**
530C	602	(Second grade paint version of 530A) (E)
535A		Cavalry service dress, peak cap (D) **263**
535B		Cavalry service dress, steel helmet (D) **263**
562A		Cowboy firing rifle (large 3¹/₂" size) (C) **279**
565A		Indian with tomahawk (large 3¹/₂" size) (C) **279**
569A	70	Roman gladiator (E) **281**
569G		Roman warrior, gilt (D)
575A		Khaki officer, peak cap (large 3¹/₂" size) (C) **279**
575B		Khaki infantry, steel helmet (large 3¹/₂" size) (C) **279**
577A		Crusader (large 3¹/₂" size) also issued in gilt (C) **279**
581		Roman chariot and charioteer (D) **281**
583		As 581, gilt paint (D)
589A		Mounted cowboy (small scale) (D) **316**
590A		Mounted Indian with tomahawk (small scale) (D) **316**
591		Police speed cop (C) **290**
591D		Khaki despatch rider, peak cap (C) **263**
592		Police motor cycle and sidecar combination (C) **290**
593AC		Khaki infantry at slope, peak cap, bandolier (D) **263**
594C		Khaki infantry at slope, peak cap (D) **263**
605		Station truck (D)
611	K70	Khaki, steel helmet, standing colour bearer (D) **263**
614	K67	Kneeling machine gunner (E) **263**
614A	K67	As 614, plain casting (E)
614P	K67	(Second grade paint version of 614) (E)
615		Prone machine gunner, peak cap (D) **263**
615A		As 615, casting only (D)
615P		(Second grade paint version of 615) (D)
632P		—
632C		—
621P		—
621C		—
622		Cannon (C) **273**
641		—
642		—
644A		Race horse and jockey (C)
654		Beacon (C) **290**
655		Traffic light (C) **290**
656		Traffic lights/beacon (C)
665		Bus stop (C)
673		—
674		—
677	16	Sudanese Camel Corps (C) **278**
678		Bedouin Arab on camel (D) **278**
681		Nurse kneeling (D) **265**
681		Nurse standing (D) **265**
682		Doctor service dress (D) **265**
688		Policeman (B)
689		Inniskilling fusilier at slope, fixed arm (D) **268**
689C	39A	Fusilier marching at slope (second grade paint version of 689) (D)
691	19	Scots Grey, mounted trumpeter (D) **270**
691G		Mounted trumpeter, gilt (D)
692	22	Mounted Scots Grey standard bearer (issued with lead and paper flags) (D) **270**
692G		Mounted standard bearer, gilt (D)
694	612/13	Range rider with revolver, removable from horse (C) **316**
695	611/14	Range rider with rifle, removable from horse (C) **316**
696		—
697		Shell petrol pump (C) **290**
698		Dominion petrol pump (C)
699		Power petrol pump (C)
755	M30	Wild West stage coach, driver and guard (C) **320**

Pre-war	Post-war		
773	18	Royal Canadian Mounted Police, mounted (D)	**277**
902C	622	Mounted Indian, firing rifle (D)	**316**
903C	628	Mounted cowboy, firing revolver (D)	**316**
904C	610	Cowboy firing rifle over lying horse (C)	**316**
905		Policewoman (B)	**290**
906		Policeman running with truncheon (B)	**290**
907	23	Mounted Field Marshal (D)	**269**
908	53	Black Watch charging (issued also with khaki socks) (E)	**267**
909C	59	Fusilier at attention (D)	**268**
910	38	Middlesex Regiment, present arms (C)	**268**
911	34	Scots Guards, standard bearer (C)	**270**
912	56	Manchester Regiment, kneeling firing (blue helmet) (D)	**268**
913		Stretcher party, service dress (C)	**265**
914	—		
915C	57	Liverpool Regiment, standing at slope (blue helmet) (D)	**268**
916	652	Cowboy firing rifle (small size) (E)	**317**
916A	651	Cowboy firing two revolvers, small size (E)	**317**
917	658	Indian standing firing rifle (E)	**317**
917A	657	Indian kneeling firing bow (E)	**317**
918	62	Royal Canadian Mounted Police at ease (D)	**277, 289**
920		Wounded soldier on stretcher (C)	**265**
921		Stretcher party, full dress (B)	**265**
922		Senior medical officer, full dress (B)	
923		Junior medical officer, full dress (B)	**265**
924	13	Mounted hussar (D)	**269**
9255		Mounted 12th lancer, Prince of Wales' Royal, movable arm (D)	**269**
926		Oil cabinet (C)	**290**
931	624	Mounted cowgirl with revolver (D)	**316**
932		Mounted policeman (C)	**290**
933		Infantry prone, peak cap, lying firing (D)	**263**
934		Police van (B)	
935		Police box (B)	**290**
936		Sussex Light Infantry officer with field glasses (B)	
937		Royal Marine captain (B)	
938		Royal Marine marching at slope, movable arm (B)	**273**
939		Royal Marine bugler (B)	**273**
940		Infantry, steel helmet, khaki at slope (B)	**263, 266**
941		Infantry captain (B)	**263, 266**
942	K53	Infantry, steel helmet, kneeling gunner, gas mask (D)	**263**
943	K59	Infantry, steel helmet, standing gunner, gas mask (D)	**263**
944		Civil Air Guard instructor (B)	**273**
945		Civil Air Guard pupil (B)	**273**
946		Texas Ranger mounted, removable from horse (C)	**316**

Pre-war issues in boxed sets

(Not given individual catalogue numbers)

17/1 19/1 32/3 34/9　Black Watch at the ready (also issued in khaki) (E) **267**

19/8 34/6 34/2 38/3 68/1 96/2　Royal Scots Grey trotting (D) **270**

19/8 34/6 38/3 68/1　Royal Scots Grey trotting trumpeter (C)

Pre-war issues

(As yet no allocated catalogue numbers)

American dough boy, marching at slope (B)

French Foreign Legion, marching at slope (B)

Austro-Hungarian infantry, marching at slope (B) **276**

London Scottish, kneeling firing (C) **267**

Greek Evzone, marching at slope (C) **277**

Indian infantry, khaki, kneeling at ready (C) **277**

Khaki infantry, peak cap, order arms (B)

Japanese seated machine gunner (B)

Japanese infantry, marching at slope (C) **277**

Japanese infantry, running charging (B)

Japanese army motor cycle and rider (B) **277**

Australian infantry, khaki, running fixed bayonet (C) **277**

ATS marching (B) **263**

WAAF marching (B)

Air raid warden (or steel helmeted WW2 policeman) (B) **290**

Female air raid warden (or Auxiliary Fire Service) (B) **290**

Khaki infantry, lying firing, peak cap, feet apart (C) **263**

Home Guard, forage cap (D) **263**

Airman, forage cap (D) **273**

Khaki soldier, anti-gas suit, gas mask, litmus rag on fixed bayonet (C) **263**

RAF ground crew (B) **273**

Pilot running (C) **273**

Pilot walking (issued in khaki and white) (C) **273**

Finnish ski troop (B) **277**

Motor cycle and side car, peak cap, driver and passenger in khaki (B)

Khaki soldier, peak cap, at slope (taken from Ethiopian infantry mould), also found with red tunic (C) **263**

Sailor, blue jacket at slope (C)

Sailor, blue jacket, trail (C) **273**

Sailor, blue jacket, at slope, bandolier (see 593AC) (C) **273**

Russian infantry at slope (B) **276**

Russian cavalry (B) **276**

Italian infantry, tropical helmet (B) **265**

Ethiopian stretcher party (C) **265**

Ethiopian marching at slope (C) **265**

Ethiopian mules and handlers with gun (C) **265**

Ethiopian tribesman with musket (later issued in post-war boxed set no. 220 as Arabs) (C) **277**

Line infantry lying firing (B) **268**

Black Watch at ready (also issued in boxed sets 17/7, 19/1, 32/3, 34/9 but painted khaki) (E) **267**

Khaki soldier at slope, forage cap, greatcoat (C) **274**

Khaki soldier, peak cap, grenade (stick) thrower (D) **263**

Khaki soldier, peak cap, firing rifle (a variation of 10A) (D) **263**

Khaki soldier, steel helmet, charging (E) **274**

Nurse kneeling with bandage (B) **265**

Doctor (white-coated version of 135C Station Master) (B) **265**

Highlander, lying firing, legs crossed (E) **267**

Khaki piper (paint variation of 215P) (D) **267**

US Army, steel helmet, greatcoat, slung rifle (C) **277**

Khaki soldier, peak cap, swing rifle on back (C)

European taken from Ethiopian mule handler (C) **263**

Royal Irish Ranger, mounted (a variation of mounted hussar no. 213A) (A)

Cowboy, mounted at full gallop, movable arm (D) **316**

King George VI seated on throne (large size) (B) **285**

Bust of King George V (B) **285**

Bust of 'Our Smiling Prince' Edward VIII (B) **285**

Bust of President Hoover (B) **285**

Coronation coach, footmen, grooms, guards present arms with officer, yeoman, mounted Life Guards, Horse Guards and field marshal. Issued for 1937 Coronation and revived in the 1950s, Coronation coach and four horses (not reissued in 1950s) (D) **269, 283, 284**

Elephant running with mahout (a variation of 177P) (B) **278**

Girl in bathing costume (B) **299**

Paper boy running (C) **290**

Market gardener carrying tray of produce (B) **305**

Skater (B)

Woman's League of Health and Beauty (three poses) (B) **299**

Boy and girl on seesaw (the plank has the inscription 'to make the seesaw work gently rock the tree trunk') (C) **301**

King Neptune (C) **294**

Speedway rider and cycle (C) **299**

No.	Item	T&B	FGT	B&Sons
45	Traffic set (B)	+		
46	Fire brigade set (B)	+		
47	Donkey ride set (small) (C)	+	Hut only used as pigsty	+ Everything but hut
48	Donkey ride set (large) (C) 435	+		
49	Road cleaning set (B) 437	+	(+)	
50	Elephant large (C) 447	+	+	Elephant
51	Elephant small (D) 451	+		+
52	Camel (D) 450	+		+
53	Giraffe (D) 451	+		+
54	Lion sitting (D) 451	+	+	
55	Lioness sitting (D) 451	+		+
56	Lion cub walking (D)	+		+
57	Lion cub lying (C)	+		
58	Pelican (D) 451	+		+
59	Penguin (D) 451	+		+
60	Eagle (D) 451	+	+	New giant tortoise, (D) 454
61	Hyena (D) 451	+		+
62	Cage rails (straight) (D)	+	+	Giant tortoise ride (C) 454
63	Cage rails (curved) (D)	+	+	
64	Railing (straight) (D) 452	+		+
65	Railing (curved) (D) 452	+		+
66	Zoo gate (C) 452	+	+	
67	Paybox (C) 452	+		+
68	Turnstile (C) 452	+		+
69	Palm tree (C) 452	+		+
70	Squirrel tree (C) 451	+	+	
71	Keeper astride for elephant (D) 447	+		+
72	Keeper standing (D) 447	+	+	
73	Keeper standing with pail (D) 447	+	+	
74	Keeper with monkey in arms (C) 447, 446			+
75	Seated children (for elephant rides) (D) 447	+		+
76	Seat for elephant (D) 447	+		+
77	Camel boy (C) 450	+		+
78	Zoo visitor man (B) 450	+	(+)	
79	Zoo visitor woman (B) 450	+	(+)	
80	Zoo visitor girl (B) 450	+	(+)	
81	Steps (C) 452	+	+	
82	Brown bear sitting (D)	+		
83	White bear sitting (D) 451	+		+ 89
84	Brown bear walking (D)	+		+ 82 / Sitting and cub +
85	White bear walking (D) 451	+		
86	Brown bear cub walking (D)	+	+	Allocated to owl 423
87	Brown bear cub begging (D)	+		+
87a	White bear cub begging (D) 451	+		+
88a	White bear cub walking (D) 451	+	+	88
88	Stag (D) 451	+	+	
89	Tiger (D) 430	+		+
90	Lion walking (D) 451	+		+
90a	Lioness walking (D)	+	+	
91	Crocodile (D) 451	+	+	Lioness lying
92	Llama with cart (C) 449	+	+ without cart	+ governess cart
92a	Donkey with cart (C)	+	(+)	
93	Snake (D) 451	+	+	

No.	Item	T&B	FGT	B&Sons
94	Monkey sitting (D) 451	+		+
95	Monkey hanging, brown or grey (D) 451	+		+
96	Baboon (D) 451	+		+
97	Gorilla (D) 451	+	+	
98	Bison (D) 451	+		+
99	Buffalo (D) 451	+	+	
100	Hippopotamus (D) 451	+		
101	Rhinoceros (D) 451	+	+	
102				
103	Zebra (D)	+		
104	Ostrich (D) 451	+	+	
105	Llama (D) 451	+		+104
105a	Wild ass (D) 451	+		+105
106	Kangaroo (D) 451	+		+
107	Seal (D) 448	+		+
108	Zoo hostess (C)	+		+ Lady in beehive hat 450
109	Governess Cart Set (pony and two children) (C) 449			+
109a	Pony with cart (C) 449	+		109
110	Tiger lying (D) 430	+		+
111	Saloon (B)	+		Old tigerwalking 430
112	Transport (B)	+		New Shetland pony (C) 458
113	Royal Mail (B)	+		Tiger cub
114	Ambulance 'grey' (B)	+		
114a	Ambulance 'khaki' (B)	+		
115	Sports (B)	+		
116	Coupé (B)	+		
117	Ambulance 'street' (B)	+		
118	Milk supply (B)	+		
119	Racer (B)	+		+
120	Fire engine (C)	+		+
121	Vacuum cleaner (D) 443	+		+
122	Butter dish and knife (C)	+		Telephone + Dinner set
123	Aeroplane Atlanta training plane (B)	+		+ Jug and basin
124	Airmail van (B)	+		New cat and kitten set (C) 460
125	Jug and basin (E) 459	+		
126	Gas stove and dolls' house cutlery (C)	+		New cat lying (C) 460
127	Gas stove (C) 443			+
127a	Gas stove (C) 443			+
128	Tanker (B)	+		New dog and kennel (C) 460
129	Breakdown lorry (B)	+		New kennel 460
130	Petrol pumps (C) 459	+		+
131	Fireplace and curb (B) 442	+		Telephone, new style 442, 459
132	Companion set (B)	+		
133	Fire screen (B)	+		Pails
134	Coal vase (B)	+		
135	Firemen (assorted) (C) 457	+		+
136	Fire escape (C)	+		+
137	DH Comet (B)	+		+
138	Air mail streamline (B)	+		
139	Saloon (B)	+		

No.	Description	T&B	FGT	B&Sons
140	Traffic beacon (C) **459**	+	+	
141	Traffic signal (D) **459**	+		+ Traffic lights, new style (D) **459**
142	Traffic policeman (D) **457**	+		+
143	Policeman mounted (D) **457**	+		+
144	Safety island (C) **459**	+		+
145	Traffic signs (D) **459**	+	+30mph	
146	Electric pumps (D) **459**	+	+	
147	Ladies (D) **457**	+		+
148	Gents (D) **457**	+	+	New man (C) **457**
149	Children hand in hand (C) **450**	+		+
150	Pavement section (C)	+		
151	Pavement corner section (C)	+		
152	Motor coach, streamline (B)	+		Pillar box set + pillar box, new style (C)
153	Brickwork pillars (C) **457**	+		
154	Brickwork and hedge (C) **457**	+		
155	Brickwork and railings (C) **457**	+		
156	Oil pump cabinet (D) **461**	+	+	New ducks (C) **460**
157	HM letterbox (C)	+	+	New drakes (C) **460**
158	HM letterbox, airmail (C)	+	+	New Duck and nest Set (C) **460**
159	Postman (C) **457**	+		+ New postman (C) **457**
160	Air pilot (D) **457**	+		+
161	Mechanic (D) **457**	+		+ **572**
162	Chauffeur (C) **457**	+	(+)	New swan (C) **458**
163	Fire engine, streamline (C)	+		New cygnet (C) **458**
164	Fire engine set (C)	+		New lamb (D) **458**
165	Tree (D) **452**	+		+
166	Bush (D) **430**	+		+
167	Fence (D) **464**	+		+
168	Gate (D) **464**	+		+
169	Cow bellowing (C) **458**	+	+	
170	Bull (D) **458**	+	+	
171				
172	Farmer (D) **457**	+		+
173	Cowman (D) **457**	+	+	
174	Milkmaid (D) **457**	+		+
175	Well (D) **464**	+		+
176	Water pump (C) **464**	+	+	
177	Cow grazing (D) **458**	+		+
178	Cow lying (D) **458**	+		+
179	Pig (E) **458**	+		+
180	Sheep standing (E) **458**	+	+	
181	Stile (E) **464**	+	+	+
182	Trough (E)	+		+
183	Stork (D) **451**	+		+
184	Sheep grazing (E) **458**	+		+
185	Piglet (E)	+		+
186	Owl (D) **461**	+		86

No.	Description	T&B	FGT	B&Sons
187	Parrot (C) **451**	+		+
188	Horse (E) **458**	+		+
189	Colt (E) **458**	+		+ 186
190	Maid and lamb (C) **457**	+	+	New Calf lying (D) **458**
191	Sheep lying (E) **458**	+		+
192	Calf standing (E) **158**	+		+
193	Deck chair (B) **459**	+		New Land girl (D) **458**
194	Donkey (D) **435**	+		+
195	Baby donkey (D) **435**	+		+
196	Farm wagon and load (B)	+		New Bee hive (C) **462**
197	Trolley bus, small (B)	+		New Turkey (D) **458**
200	Air and water tower (B) **462**	+		New Dog lying (D) **460**
201	Gas fire (E) **442**	+		Dog **458**
202	Sentry box (E) **439**	+	+	New Rabbit burrow set (C) **460**
203	Not yet identified (E)			
204	Trolley bus, large (B)	+		
205				
−209	Not yet identified (E)			
210	WATS (marching and bugler) (B) **444**	+	(+)	
211	First aid (stretcher party) (B) **442, 444**	+	(+)	
212	Trailer pump (3 figures & pump) (C) **444**	+	(+)	
213	Decontamination squad (five figures) (B) **444**	+	(+)	
214	Stirrup pump (five figures) (B) **444**	+	(+)	
215				
−221	Not yet identified (E)			
222	Washing machine (D) **443**			+
223				
224	Refrigerator (D) **443**	+		+
300	Hunting crocodile (B)	+		
301	Pedestrian set (C)	+		
302	Covered wagon (B) **438**	+		
303	Indian and canoe set (C) **438**	+		+
304	Sledge and dogs (B) **436**	+	(+)	
305	Fur trappers and wolves (B) **436**	+	(+)	
306	Aeroplane set (B)	+		
307	Fire Brigade set (small) (B)	+		
308	Goblin cleaner (D)	+	(+)	
309	Canoe Set (small) (C) **438**	+	(+)	
310	Rickshaw set with Zulu or Chinese coolee (B) **433**	+	(+)	
311	Trailer pump in action with firemen (B) **444**	+	+	
500	Fir tree, small (C) **436**	+	+	
500	Fir tree, large (C) **436**	+	+	
502	Indian canoe (C) **438**	+		+
503	Indian paddle right (C) **438**	+		+
503	Indian paddle left (C) **438**	+		+
504	Indian crawling (D) **438**	+		+
505	Indian running (D) **438**	+		+
506	Mounted Indian chief (D) **438**	+		+
—	Indian campfire (B) **438**	+		
—	Cowboy, mounted (C) **438**	+		+ 505
—	Cowgirl, mounted (C) **438**	+		+ 506
—	Mounted Indian on frisky horse (B) **438**	+		

		T&B	FGT	B&Sons
—	Mounted Indian galloping, firing rifle (D) **438**	+		
—	Cowboy firing rifle (C) **438**	+		
—	Mounted cowboy firing pistol (C) **438**	+		
1500	Khaki infantry (set of six) (B)	+		
1501	The Buffs (set of six) (B)	+		
1502	The Grenadiers (set of six) (B)	+		
1503	The Gordon Highlanders (set of six) (B)			
—	Slope and officer with sword (B)	+		
2000	Hussars (set of four) (B) **440, 439**	+		
2001	Cavalry and foot (set of four) (B)	+		
2002	Display Set, khaki at slope, sailors and dragoons (B) **441**	+		
—	Dragoons (B) **439**	+		
2010	Barbed wire entanglement (C) **439**	+		+
2014	Changing guard (large set) (B)	+		
2014	Changing guard (small set) (B)	+		
2016	Attack (B)	+		
3500	Highlanders (B) **439**	+		+
3501	The Buffs (B) **439**	+		+
3502	Grenadiers walking (D) **439**	+		+

		T&B	FGT	B&Sons
3503	Grenadiers at attention (D) **439**	+		+
3504	Sailor (C) **439**	+		+
3505	Naval guard (C) **439**	+		Lifeboat man
3506	Naval officer (C) **439**	+	+	Lancer
3507	Royal Marines (C) **439**	+		Scots Grey
3508	Lifeboat man (C) **440**	+		+ Hussar 3505
3509	Naval diver (B) **440**	+	+	Life Guard
3510	Sussex infantry (B) **439**			+
—	Marine (C)			3511
—	Mounted guardsman, pre-war? (B)			
—	Man with two buckets (C) **444**	+		Post-war zoo keeper with fish (C) **447**

Appliances and utensils

	T&B/FGT/B&Sons		
Gas fire (C) **442**			
Gas fire with tiled surround (C) **442**	Electric fire with plug (C) **442**		
Telephone, upright (C) **442**	Electric fire (C) **442**		
Radiator (C) **442**	Iron (C) **442, 459**		

A BARRETT & SONS

Some items listed and illustrated are new figures, produced post-war and designed by Barrett & Sons. In some cases the catalogue reference number is new, in others the catalogue number given is the original Taylor & Barrett number, re-allocated to the new Barrett & Sons product. By cross checking the master Taylor & Barrett list, comparisons in relation to Barrett & Sons products can be drawn. Moulds and castings previously issued by Taylor & Barrett, but inherited and issued by Barrett & Sons are not listed here and can be found in the Taylor & Barrett check list.

13   Elephant ride, howdah, two children, seated keeper. (The elephant is the only new item in this set. F G Taylor inherited the Taylor & Barrett elephant, Barrett & Sons the howdah keeper and children.) (C) **447, 453**

13a   Elephant ride, small (C)

21   Camel ride (C) **450**

25   Schoolmaster and easel (pre-war allocated to telephone) (C) **462**

33   Chicken sets, white, brown or black (pre-war allocated to Jazz Band) (C) **460**

34   Chickens (pre-war allocated to lion hunt) (D) **460**

60   Giant tortoise (pre-war allocated to eagle) (D) **454**

62   Giant tortoise ride and girl (pre-war allocated to curved rail) (C) **454**

73   Keeper walking with fish and pail (C) **447**

91   Lioness lying (pre-war allocated to crocodile) (D)

112   Shetland pony (pre-war allocated to motor vehicles) (C) **458**

113   Tiger cub (pre-war allocated to motor vehicles) (C)

125   Cat in basket with kittens (pre-war allocated to Jug and Basin set) (C) **460**

126   Cat lying (pre-war allocated to gas stove) (C) **460**

128   Dog, puppies and kennel set (pre-war allocated to tanker) (E) **460**

129   Kennel (pre-war allocated to breakdown lorry) (D) **460**

133   Pails (pre-war allocated to fire screen) (D)

143   Mounted Police (D)

148   Gentleman in raincoat and cap, carrying umbrella (new figure) (C) **457**

156   Ducks (pre-war allocated to oil pump cabinet) (C) **460**

157   Drakes (pre-war allocated to letter box) (C) **460**

158   Ducks in nest set (pre-war allocated to air mail letter box) (C) **460**

159   Postman with letter (new version using old reference number) (C) **457**

162   Swan (pre-war allocated to chauffeur) (C) **458**

163   Cygnet (pre-war allocated to fire engine) (C) **458**

164   Lamb (pre-war allocated to fire engine set) (D) **458**

169   Cow standing (pre-war allocated to cow bellowing) (D) **458**

180   Goat (pre-war allocated to sheep standing) (D) **458, 418**

186   Colt (pre-war allocated to owl) (D) **458**

190   Calf lying (pre-war allocated to maid and lamb) (D) **458**

193   Landgirl with two buckets (pre-war allocated to deck chair) (D) **458**

196   Beehive (pre-war allocated to wagon and load) (C) **462**

197   Turkey (pre-war allocated to trolley bus) (D) **458**

198   Rabbit running (new figure) (C) **460**

199   Rabbit sitting with carrot (new figure) (C) **460**

200   Dog lying (pre-war) (D) **458, 460**

201   Dog standing (pre-war allocated to gas fire) (C) **458**

202   Rabbit, baby rabbits and burrow set (pre-war allocated to sentry box) (C) **460**

334   Chicken set in egg cup (new figure) (C) **460**

521   Pixie tree house set (B) **461**

522   Pixie tea party (B) **461**

524   Walking pixie (B) **461**

525   Seated pixie (B) **461**

526   Pixie seated on toadstool (B) **461**

527   Pixie waiter with tray (B) **461**

531   Toadstool table (B) **461**

571   Petrol pumps (C) **462**

573   Motor cyclist (B)

600   Lake set (B)

601   Petrol pumps (D) **462**

603   Oil cabinet (D) **462**

604   Air and water (D) **462**

607   Safety island (C) **459**

612   Trolley bus (B)

615   Traffic lights (D) **459**

—   Tiger lying (new figure) (C)

—   Tiger cub (new figure) (C)

—   Coronation coach (E)

—   Standing keeper (new figure) (C) **447**

—   Standing keeper converted from postman (C) **447**

—   Spaceship (A) **463**

F G TAYLOR & SONS

The figures listed are those designed and issued post-war by F G Taylor & Sons. The firm did not use a catalogue number reference. The numbers on the left indicate which items were redesigned from the Taylor & Barrett range.

52   Camel walking (pre-war allocated to camel standing) (C) **456**

59   Penguin (D)

71   Seated keeper (D) **447**

83   White bear sitting, also issued in brown (D) **456**

85   Bear walking, white or brown (D) **456**

88a   Bear cub walking, white or brown (D) **456**

89   Tiger walking (D) **456**

90   Lion walking (B) **598**

90a   Lioness walking, same casting as 89 and 90 (D) **456**

105	Llama (D) **598**
106	Kangaroo (D) **456**
107	Seal (D)
175	Well (D) **464**
177	Cow grazing (D)
178	Cow lying (D) **458**
179	Pig (E)
182	Trough (E)
184	Sheep grazing (E)
185	Piglet (E)
191	Sheep lying (E) **458**
192	Calf walking (E) **458**
—	Keeper walking empty handed (C) **447**
—	Sealion (D)
—	Baby camel (B) **456**
—	Two parrots on perch (C) **450**
—	Goat (D) **458**
—	Wolf howling (C) **436**
—	Wolf with lolling tongue (C) **436**

(The above two items were previously issued pre-war only for T & B Trapper's Set)

—	Traffic lights (movable) (D) **459**
—	Duck pond (B)
—	Blacksmith's set, blacksmith, anvil, horse with leg raised, forge (C) **466**
—	Rustic bridge (D) **464**
—	Water wheel (B) **464**
—	Cottage (C) **464**
—	Windmill (D) **466**
—	Rabbit hutch and rabbits (D) **464**
—	Hen coop and brooding hen (D) **464**
—	Dovecote and dove (C) **464**
—	Shire-horse (C) **458**
—	Cob (D) **458**
—	Ivy and Brumas (B)
—	Hansom trap (farmer's gig) with farmer (B) **464**
—	Farm cart and trotting horse (C) **464**
—	State landau (B) **468**
—	Mobile animal trailer and vet (B) **467**
—	Chicks on base (D) **458**
—	Ducks on base (D) **458**
—	Wheat sheaves (D) **458**
—	Hen pecking (D) **458**
—	Hen feeding (D)
—	Hay rick (D) **464**
—	Corn rick (D) **464**
—	Scarecrow (C) **457**
—	Cockerel (D)
—	Rustic fence (D) **464**
—	Colt (D)
—	Bus stops (D) **459**
—	Traffic island (C) **459**

TIMPO

1946–1950

Arctic Set

| Sledge pulled by dogs (C) | Man with whip (C) |
| Man with slung rifle (C) | Man firing rifle (C) |

| Igloo (C) | Polar bear (C) |
| Penguin (C) | Hedges covered in snow (C) |

Boxed set (C) **470**

Although issued in Timpo boxes, it is certain that these items were manufactured pre-war by Stoddart. Several different boxed sets are known to exist, containing various combinations of the above.

Farm Set

Milkmaid (D)	Five bar fence (D)
Feeding trough (D)	Bench (D)
Horse (D)	Hedge (D)
Foal (D)	Kid (D)
Duck swimming (D)	Cockerel (D)

Boxed set (D) **471**

This is only one of several combination boxes of farm items that were issued prior to the standardisation of the Timpo range in 1950. The contents are a curious mixture. The milkmaid is by Stoddart, the hedge section is by Timpo, the cockerel and duck are of unknown manufacture, the five bar fence does not match the fence shown in any of the Timpo catalogues. The horse is marked Timpo Toys and the bench and trough seem to be Timpo also. A Crescent calf together with a Stoddart kid and a foal by unknown manufacturers makes the identification of Timpo boxed sets from this era almost impossible to document.

Ranch set

Mountain cowboy firing rifle (D)
Mounted cowboy (removable) with lasso (D)
Cowboy with two pistols (D)
Cowboy surrendering (D)
Indian chief (D)
Small bush (D)
Hedge (D)

Boxed set (E) **474**

Again, a curious combination of figures was put together to form the ranch set. The mounted cowboy with rifle and Indian Chief are by Hill and the two cowboys on foot are by Stoddart. The mounted cowboy with cast lasso seems to have been copied from the moulds used by Tudor Rose, a firm who issued hard plastic figures during the late 1940s and early 1950s. The hedge and bush were Timpo products.

Zoo set

Giraffe (C)	Elephant (C)	Gorilla (C)
Leopard (C)	Lion (C)	Stag (C)
Doe (C)	Donkey (C)	Penguin (C)
Sea lion (C)	Bear (C)	Polar bear (C)
Camel (C)	Palm tree (C)	Shrub (C)

Boxed set (C) **473**

The first animals listed are not standard Timpo issues but probably Stoddart.

Happy Hunting Series

A combination of former Kew products. Mounted huntsmen and huntswomen, fox and hounds.

Boxed set (C) **472**

Garage Set

Kneeling mechanic (C)	Standing mechanic (C)
Shell petrol pump (C)	Power petrol pump (C)
Various die-cast vehicles (C)	

Boxed set (C) **512**

The following items were die-cast:

Mechanic, hands on hips, 40mm (C) **512**
Mechanic lying, 40mm (C) **512**

The petrol pumps and mechanics are marked 'Timpo Toys' and are usually found in boxed sets marked 'Made in Eire'. These sets are probably the only items released by the two 'breakaway' directors, Hyland and Kiernan, who set up in Eire as Timpo Toys Limited

Composition figures

Chauffeur (B) **476**
Mechanic standing (C) **512**
Mechanic kneeling (C) **512**
Airman (D) **505**
Khaki infantry, steel helmet (D)
Khaki infantry, tropical helmet (D)
Airman (small scale) (C)

1950–1955

British khaki infantry

1	Kneeling firing (C) **505**
2	Standing firing (C) **505**
3	Lying firing (C) **505**
4	Standing firing (C) **505**
5	Crawling (C) **505**
6	Grenade thrower (C) **505**
7	Officer (D) **505**
8	Charging with fixed bayonet (C) **505**
9	Charging (C) **505**
10	Stabbing downwards (C) **505**

Farm Series

MF1000	Cow standing (D) **479**
MF1001	Cow mooing (D) **479**
MF1002	Cow feeding (D) **479**
MF1003	Bull standing (D) **479**
MF1004	Shire-horse standing (D) **479**
MF1005	Shire-horse feeding (D) **479**
MF1006	Horse standing (D) **479**
MF1007	Shire colt (D) **479**
MF1008	Calf standing (E) **479**
MF1009	Calf head turned (E) **479**
MF1010	Sheep standing (E) **479**
MF1011	Sheep feeding (E) **479**
MF1012	Sheep lying (E) **479**
MF1013	Lamb (E) **479**
MF1014	Sheep dog (D) **477**
MF1015	Goat (D) **479**

MF1016 Pig standing (E) **479**
MF1017 Sow with piglets (D) **479**
MF1018 Piglets (E) **479**
MF1019 Goose (E) **479**
MF1020 Gander (E) **479**
MF1021 Cockerel (E) **479**
MF1022 Chicken standing (E) **479**
MF1023 Chicken feeding (E) **479**
MF1024 Hen brooding (E) **479**
MF1025 Chicks (two on a base) (E) **479**
MF1026 Man with wheelbarrow (C) **477**
MF1027 Man haymaker (E) **477**
MF1028 Drover (E) **477**
MF1029 Shepherd (D) **477**
MF1030 Milkmaid milking (E) **477**
MF1031 Milkmaid walking (E) **477**
MF1032 Woman haymaking (E) **477**
MF1033 Woman feeding chicks (E) **477**
MF1034 Scarecrow (E) **477**
MF1035 Hurdle (E) **479**
MF1036 Trough (E) **479**
MF1037 Bench (E) **479**
MF1038 Hedge and bush (D) **479**
MF1039 Tree (C) **477**
MF1040 —
MF1041 Bucket (C)
MF1042 Milk churn (C) **479**
MF1043 Large tree (C) **477**
MF1044 Small tree (C)
MF1045 Gander wild (D) **479**
MF1046 Donkey (D) **479**
MF1047 Farmer leading bull **(C) 477**
MF1048 Turkey hen (C) **479**
MF1049 Turkey cock (E) **479**
— Well (B) **477**
— Dog in orange collar (C) **479**

Horse-drawn farm vehicles
Farm cart (B)
Water cart (B) **480**
Log wagon pulled by two horses (B) **480**
Farm roller and driver (B)
Farm harrow and driver (B)
Driver (B) **477**

Although issued in boxed sets, the following items were not allocated individual catalogue numbers:

Foal with head and tail raised (D) **523**
Calf lying (E) **523**
Dog with orange collar (D) **479**

Wild West Series
WW2000 Mounted cowboy with two guns (D) **483**
WW2001 Mounted cowboy with pistol and rifle (D) **483**
WW2002 Buffalo Bill mounted with lasso (D) **482**
WW2003 Mounted sheriff with whip (D) **483**
WW2004 Mounted cowboy with lasso (D) **483**
WW2005 Mounted cowboy, hands bound (D) **483**
WW2006 Mounted cowboy mopping brow (fatigued) (D) **483**
WW2007 Mounted cowboy lassoing wild horse (D) **483**

WW2008 Mounted cowboy surrendering (D) **483**
WW2009 Mounted cowboy with rifle, bandaged head (D) **483**
WW2010 Mounted Indian chief with shield (D) **483**
WW2011 Mounted cowboy firing rifle (D) **483**
WW2012 Cowboy tied to tree (C) **484**
WW2013 Mounted Indian chief with bow and arrow (D) **483**
WW2014 Mounted Indian chief with spear (D) **483**
WW2015 Indian brave with bow and arrow (D) **484**
WW2016 Indian brave kneeling with bow and arrow (D) **484**
WW2017 Seated cowboys with accordion and guitar with camp fire (C) **484**
WW2018 Indian chief crawling (D) **484**
WW2019 Indian brave running with spear (E) **484**
WW2020 Canadian Mounted Policeman (C) **484**
WW2021 Seated Indian brave with large tom-tom (D) **484**
WW2022 Seated Indian brave with small tom-tom (C) **484**
WW2023 Indian chief walking with spear (D) **484**
WW2024 Indian brave advancing with rifle (D) **484**
WW2025 Indian chief standing with spear (D) **484**
WW2026 Indian chief sitting (C) **484**
WW2027 Sheriff standing (D) **484**
WW2028 'Timpo Tim' (D) **484**
(Timpo launched a promotional scheme in March 1950 in the form of a comic named *Pioneer Western*. This featured 'The Adventures of Timpo Tim – US Ranger'.)
WW2029 'Slim' (D) **484**
WW2030 Bandit firing to the right (D) **484**
WW2031 Bandit firing two pistols to the left (D) **484**
WW2032 Cowboy with US mail bag (D) **484**
WW2033 Squaw (D) **484**
WW2034 Cowboy tied to wooden tree trunk (B) **484**

Other Wild West items
MZ4028 Texas longhorn. (This item from the Zoo Series was issued in Wild West boxed display sets) (C) **483**
— Wild West wagon with two horses and cowboy driver with whip. (The horses are those listed under WW2007 with added harness) (B) **481**
— Corral fence (D) **479**

The official 'Hopalong Cassidy' Western Series
2100 Hopalong standing (C) **482**
2101 Hopalong (no hat) fighting (C) **482**
2102 Lucky (C) **482**
2103 California (C) **482**
2104 Hopalong mounted (C) **482**
2105 Lucky mounted (C) **482**
2106 California mounted (C) **482**

Boxed display sets were supplemented by cowboys from the Wild West Series. During the early 1950s display boxes containing Timpo, Benbros, Harvey and Hill cowboys and Indians were commissioned by the Woolworth department store chain.

Guardsmen, Life Guards, Horse Guards and Highlanders
3000 Guards drum major marching (E) **501**
3001 Guards fifer marching (D) **501**

3002 Guards side drummer marching (D) **501**
3003 Guards cymbals marching (D) **501**
3004 Guards standard bearer standing (D) **501**
3005 Guards bugler marching (D) **501**
3006 Guards trombone marching (D) **501**
3007 Guards bass drummer (removable drum) (D) **501**
3008 Guards officer marching, drawn sword (D) **504**
3009 Guardsman presents arms (E) **504**
3010 Guardsman marching at slope (D) **504**
3011 Guardsman standing firing (E) **504**
3012 Guardsman keeling firing (E) **504**
3013 Guardsman lying firing (D) **504**
3014 Guards tuba marching (D) **501**
3015 Royal Horse Guard standing attention (C) **504**
3016 Mounted Royal Horse Guard officer (D) **504**
3017 Mounted Royal Horse Guard (C) **504**
3018 Highland officer marching, drawn sword (E) **504**
3019 Highlander marching at slope (D) **504**
3020 Highland piper (D) **504**
Numbers 3015, 3017, and 3017 were also issued as Life Guards (E) **514**
Guardsmen and Highlanders were also issued with flock coated busbies.

Model Zoo Series
MZ4000 Elephant (D) **486**
MZ4001 Baby Elephant (D) **485**
MZ4002 Camel (D) **485**
MZ4003 Giraffe (D) **485, 487**
MZ4004 Hippopotamus (D) **485**
MZ4005 Rhinoceros (D) **485, 487**
MZ4006 Lion lying (D) **485**
MZ4007 Lioness (D) **485**
MZ4008 Tiger (D) **485**
MZ4009 Monkey with ball (D) **514**
MZ4010 Monkey on tree (D) **485, 487**
MZ4011 Mountain goat (D) **485, 487**
MZ4012 Stag (D) **485, 487**
MZ4013 Polar bear standing (D) **485**
MZ4014 Brown bear walking (D) **485**
MZ4015 Polar bear baby standing (D) **485**
MZ4016 Kangaroo (D) **485**
MZ4017 Sea lion (D) **485**
MZ4018 Tortoise (D) **485, 487**
MZ4019 Crocodile (D) **485, 487**
MZ4020 Squirrel on branch (C) **485**
MZ4021 Zebra (D) **485, 487**
MZ4022 Penguin (D) **485**
MZ4023 Stork (D) **485, 487**
MZ4024 Ostrich (D) **485, 487**
MZ4025 Pelican (D) **485, 487**
MZ4026 Eagle (D) **485**
MZ4027 Bison (D) **486**
MZ4028 Texas longhorn (C) **483**
MZ4029 Indian water buffalo (C) **485**
MZ4050 Zoo keeper carrying two buckets (D) **486**
MZ4051 Zoo inspector (D) **486**
MZ4052 Zoo keeper with brush (D) **486, 487**
MZ4060 Zoo cage in six sections (C) **486**

Numbers MZ4013 and MZ4015 were also issued as brown bears while MZ4014 was also issued as a polar bear (D) **485**

Ivy and Brumas (numbers MZ4014 and MZ4015) were issued in a boxed set to celebrate the birth of the baby polar bear Brumas at London Zoo. (B) **485**

Farm trees numbered MF1043 were issued in some of the boxed zoo display sets.

The following were issued flock-coated: MZ4000, 4001, 4002, 4003, 4006, 4007, 4008, 4013, 4014, 4016, 4021, 4027 and 4028.

Other animals available flock-coated are listed as Indian tiger, Indian elephant trunk down and small zoo elephant, none of which are illustrated in the Timpo catalogue.

Knights in armour

KN 50	Mounted knight with sword (D)	**488**
KN 51	Mounted knight with spear (D)	
KN 52	Mounted knight with open visor (D)	**488**
KN 53	Standing knight with spear (D)	**488**
KN 54	Standing knight with sword above head (D)	**488**

Ivanhoe series
(based on the MGM film of 1953)

KN 55	Ivanhoe mounted (the Black Knight) (C)	**489**
KN 56	Sir de Bois-Guilbert mounted (C)	**489**
KN 57	Sir Hugh de Bracy mounted (C)	
KN 58	Front de Boeuf mounted (C)	
KN 59	Philip de Malvoisin mounted (C)	
KN 60	Ralph de Vipont mounted (C)	**489**
KN 61	Crusader mounted (C)	**489**

King Arthur and Knights of the Round Table
(based on the MGM film of 1954)

KN 70	Sir Lancelot mounted (D)	**491**
KN 71	Sir Mordred mounted (D)	**491**
KN 72	Sir Percival mounted (D)	**491**
KN 73	Sir Gareth mounted (D)	**491**
KN 74	Sir Gawaine mounted (D)	**491**
KN 75	Sir Agravaine mounted (D)	**491**
KN 76	Sir Bedivere mounted (D)	**491**
KN 77	Green knight mounted (D)	**491**
KN78	King Arthur mounted (D)	**491**
KN 79	Sir Lancelot on foot (D)	**491**
KN 80	Sir Mordred on foot (D)	**491**
KN 81	Simon on foot (D)	**491**
KN 82	Lambert on foot (D)	**491**
KN 83	King Arthur on foot (D)	**491**

Quentin Durward Series

HF 500	Quentin Durward mounted (C)	**492**
HF 501	Phillip de Creville mounted (C)	**492**
HF 502	Duke's guard mounted (C)	**492**
HF 503	Duke's guard standing with lance (C)	**492**
HF 504	Phillip de Creville on foot (C)	**492**
HF 505	Quentin Durward on foot (C)	**492**
HF 506	William de la Marck on foot (C)	**492**
HF 507	Gluckmeister with mechanical weapon (C)	**492**
HF 508	Landsknecht with rifle (C)	**492**
HF 509	Landsnecht with crossbow (C)	**492**
HF 510	Royal Guard standing (C)	**492**

Model dogs – 'My Pets' Series
(Individually boxed)

5000	Great Dane (C)	**493**
5001	Borzoi (C)	**493**
5002	Alsatian standing (C)	**493**
5003	Alsatian lying (C)	**493**
5004	St Bernard (D)	**493**
5005	Greyhound (C)	**493**
5006	Pointer (D)	**493**
5007	French poodle (D)	**493**
5008	Chow (E)	**493**
5009	Cocker spaniel (E)	**493**
5010	Fox terrier (E)	**493**
5011	Welsh terrier (C)	**493**
5012	Scottish terrier (E)	**493**
5013	Boston terrier (E)	**493**
5014	Bull terrier (E)	**493**
5015	Bulldog (D)	**493**
5016	Dachshund (D)	**493**
5017	Pekingese (E)	**493**

Number 5012 was also available in white depicting a West Highland white terrier, while 5009 can also be found painted as a springer (D) **493**.

The firm of Laing Products was responsible for flock-coating the above and Timpo issued them under the name Timmee Toys (see illustrated advertisement).

Footballers

6050	Shooting (C)	**495**
6051	Running (C)	**495**
6052	Standing (C)	**495**
6053	Walking (C)	**495**
6054	Goalkeeper diving (C)	**495**

Issued as individual items and in boxed sets of eleven under the title 'My Favourite Team'. The following team colours are known to have been produced after the discovery of a sample box containing various team colours: Blackburn Rovers, Blackpool, Burnley, Bolton Wanderers, Manchester United, Manchester City, Chelsea, Preston North End, Newcastle United, West Bromwich Albion, Arsenal, Wolverhampton Wanderers.

Circus Series

6100	Clown conducting with baton (C)	**498**
6101	Clown playing oboe (C)	**498**
6102	Clown playing accordion (C)	**498**
6103	Clown playing fiddle (C)	**498**
6104	Ringmaster (D)	**498**
6105	Circus horse (C)	**498**
6106	Bareback rider (C)	**498**

A circus cage on wheels and a trapeze set have recently come to light (C) **496, 497**

| 6000 | Gypsy or organ grinder with bear (C) | **498** |

(This item was also issued in circus display boxed sets as were the lion, tiger and sea lion from the Zoo Series.)

Police Force

6150	Traffic policeman (D)	**499**
6151	Standing policeman (D)	**499**
6152	Walking policeman (D)	**499**
6153	Police Inspector (D)	**499**
6154	Mobile policeman on motorcycle (C)	**499**
6155	Mounted policeman (C)	**499**
6156	Police woman (D)	**499**

An uncatalogued standing policeman with only one hand behind his back has been found. This could be a prototype never put into production (E) **499**

West Point Cadets

7000	Drum major (C)	**501**
7001	Fifer (C)	**501**
7002	Side drummer (C)	**501**
7003	Cymbals (C)	**501**
7004	Bugler (C)	**501**
7005	Trumpet (C)	**501**
7006	Trombone (C)	**501**
7007	Tuba (C)	**501**
7008	Bass drummer (C)	**501**
7009	Standard bearer (C)	**500**
7010	Officer with drawn sword (C)	**500**
7011	Present arms (C)	**500**
7012	Marching at slope (C)	**500**
7013	At ease (C)	**500**
7014	Standing firing (C)	**500**
7015	Kneeling firing (C)	**500**
7016	Mounted on white horse (B)	**500**
7017	Officer walking (C)	**500**
7018	Officer saluting (C)	**500**
7019	Officer at ease (C)	**500**

The original series was issued in blue tunics which resembled the citadel of South Carolina rather than West Point Cadets. Timpo did change the tunic colours to grey during the latter part of their production. These second version figures are rare. (B)

Railway Series

8000	Station master (D)	**508**
8001	Railway guard (D)	**508**
8002	Railway signalman (C)	**508**
8003	Railway porter with barrow (D)	**508**
8004	Railway porter with luggage (C)	**508**
8005	Railway porter with whistle (D)	**508**
8006	Mother with child (C)	**508**
8007	Girl (C)	**508**
8008	Boy (C)	**508**
8009	Sailor with kit bag (B)	**508**
8010	Soldier with kit bag (B)	**508**
8011	Hiker (B)	**508**
8012	Commercial traveller (C)	**508**
8013	Businessman (C)	**508**
8014	Mr Brown (C)	**508**
8015	Mrs Green (C)	**508, 510**
8016	Mr Smith (C)	**508**
8017	Mrs Smith (C)	**508**

Several railway personnel were issued as Negroes in red caps for the US market (E) **503**. Some of the passengers from this series have been found in different paint variations, e.g. Mrs Green in yellow coat. These are thought to have been specially commissioned as fair ground prizes (E) **510**.

Two figures issued in the railway range were painted in white coats to represent medical officers.

8000   Station master/doctor (B)
8008   Boy/doctor (B) **506**

Miniature Railway Series
(Semi-flat) Made in Mazak
Boxed set of 'OO' gauge station passengers and personnel (B) **511**

US Army and Navy
9000   At ease (D) **506**
9001   Marching slung rifle (D) **506**
9002   Observer with binoculars (D) **506**
9003   Mine detector and operator (D) **506**
9004   Soldier crawling (D) **506**
9005   Officer kneeling with map (D) **506**
9006   Sitting with field telephone (D) **506**
9007   Despatch rider (C) **506**
9008   Kneeling with walkie-talkie (D) **506**
9009   Officer crouching with pistol (D) **506**
9010   On guard with fixed bayonet (D) **506**
9011   Standing firing (D) **506**
9012   Mortar unit (D) **506**
9013   Charging fixed bayonet (D) **506**
9014   Grenade thrower (D) **506**
9015   Advancing tommy gunner (D) **506**
9016   Kneeling with bazooka (D) **506**
9017   Seated machine gunner (D) **506**
9018   Kneeling firing (D) **506**
9019   Lying firing (D) **506**
9020   Marching at slope ceremonial uniform (D) **505**
9021   Standard bearer ceremonial uniform (D) **505**
9022   Officer ceremonial uniform (D) **505**
9023   Sitting with washing bucket (D) **506**
9024   Stretcher party (C) **506**
9025   Walking wounded (C) **506**
9026   Kneeling with mug and sandwich (D) **506**
9027   Sailor marching (D) **505**
9028   Sailor with telescope (D) **505**
9029   Sailor at slope (D) **505**
9030   Naval officer (D) **505**
9031   *
9032   Military police (E) **506**

About one figure in each batch of one hundred was issued as a black GI.

*Number 9031 has not been allocated a description. It is possible that this was a female US Army nurse which was a grey paint version of number 6156 policewoman (B) **505, 503**.

Barbed wire entanglements, a small hut and various pieces of camouflage were issued in small boxed sets to complement the US Army range (B).

Coronation decorated lamppost (B) **516**
HM The Queen in coronation robes (C) **517**

Garage and Roadside Series
No catalogue numbers have been found for the following:

Street lamps (C) **512**
Traffic lights (D)
Traffic signs (D)
Beacons (D)
Garage hand in Lex overalls rolling tyre (C) **512**
Garage hand in Lex overalls carrying petrol can (C) **512**
Garage hand in Lex overalls lying with spanner (C) **512**
Female garage hand with open hand to hold cloth (A)
Esso petrol pump (D) **512**
Esso oil cabinet (D) **512**
Fire alarm (a former Hill item) (D) **512**
Garage hand (a paint variation of Icky from the Super Heroes set) (C)
Esso oil drum (C) **512**

Big Game Hunting Set
The following were not issued with catalogue numbers:
Large elephant running trunk up (B) **507**
Large elephant walking (B) **507**
Howdah (B) **507**
White hunter (B) **507**
Maharajah (B) **507**
Indian natives with spears (B) **507**
Indian elephant boys (B) **507**
Tigers (including wounded with spears) (B) **507**
Tigers are also to be found with flock coats (B) **507**

Coronation Issues
No catalogue numbers have been found for the following:
Mounted Guards officer (C) **504**
HM The Queen mounted in trooping the colour uniform (D) **517**
Coronation coach (B) **516**
Postillions (B) **516**
Footman (C) **516**
Groom (C) **516**
Yeomen of the Guard (C) **516**
HM The Queen mounted on walking horse (A) **518**
Mounted Horse Guard (C) **504**

Super Heroes
No catalogue numbers have been found for the following:
Captain Marvel (B) **513**
Mary Marvel (B) **513**
Captain Marvel Junior (B) **513**
Captain Midnight (B) **513**
Frogman (C) **505**
Icky (B) **513**

Tarzan Series
Tarzan issued in boxed sets with various animals from the Zoo Series (B) **514**

Beatrix Potter Series
No catalogue numbers have been found for the following:
Peter Rabbit (C) **515**
Jeremy Fisher (C) **515**
Jemima Puddleduck (C) **515**
Squirrel Nutkins (C) **515**

A game was issued in which the characters were included as unpainted castings.

WEND-AL

Farm Issues
FD1   Bull (E) **580**
FD2   Bull charging (D) **580**
FD3   Calf walking (E) **580**
FD4   Cat seated on mat (B) **580**
FD5   Cockerel (E) **580**
FD6   Cow standing (E)
FD7   Cow lying (E) **580**
FD8   Dog (D) **580**
FD9   Donkey (E) **589**
FD10   Farm horse with harness (E) **579, 580**
FD11   Farmer (D) **579**
FD12   Farmer's wife (D) **579**
FD13   Farmer's daughter (D) **579**
FD14   Feeding trough (E)
FD15   Fence (E) **580**
FD16   Foal (E) **580**
FD17   Gate (E)
FD18   Goat walking (D) **580**
FD19   Goose (E)
FD20   Guinea fowl (B)
FD21   Hedge (small) (E) **580**
FD22   Hedge (large) (E) **580**
FD24   Labourer (D) **579**
FD25   Landgirl (D) **579**
FD26   Mare (D) **580**
FD27   Milkmaid (D) **579**
FD28   Peacock (C) **592**
FD29   Pig (E) **580**
FD30   Pigeon (C) **580**
FD31   Rabbit (C) **580**
FD32   Sheep (E) **580**
FD33   Tree (4" high) (D)
FD34   Turkey (E) **580**
       Hen feeding (D) **580**
       Ram (D) **580**
       Goat feeding (D) **580**
       Chick (D) **580**
       Sheep feeding (E) **580**
       Turkey (small) (D) **580**
       French farmers (C) **579**
       Man to hold pitchforks (B) **579**
       Man pushing barrow (D) **579**
       Horse-drawn harrow (D) **579**
       Horse-drawn rubber tyred rake (C) **579**
       Horse-drawn spoke wheel rake (D)
       Horse-drawn tumbril (D) **579**
       Horse-drawn plough (D) **580**
       Horse-drawn grass cutter (C)

Wild animals
W1   Bison (E) **592**
W2   Brown bear (D)
W3   Camel (one hump) (E) **592**
W4   Camel (two humps) (E) **592**
W5   Crocodile (D) **592**
W6   Elephant (D) **587**

W7   Gazelle (D) **592**
W8   Giraffe (D) **592**
W9   Gorilla (D) **592**
W10   Hippopotamus (D) **592**
W11   Kangaroo (E)
W12   Lion (E) **592**
W13   Lioness (E) **592**
W14   Monkey sitting (C) **592**
W15   Monkey walking (D) **592**
W16   Ostrich (large) (E) **592**
W17   Panda (E) **592**
W18   Panther (D) **592**
W19   Pelican (D) **592**
W20   Penguin (E) **592**
W21   Polar bear sitting (E) **592**
W22   Polar bear walking (E) **592**
W23   Rhinoceros (D) **592**
W24   Seal (D) **592**
W25   Tiger (D) **592**
W26   Zebra (E) **592**
       Baby Elephant (D) **592**
       Stork (D)
       Wolf (D)
       Turtle (D)
       Wild boar (D) **592**
       Ostrich (small) (D) **592**
       Eagle (D) **592**

Military
M1   Coldstream Guard at slope (two versions) (E) **581**
M2   Coldstream Guards officer (two versions) (E) **581**
M3   Highlander at slope (two versions) (D) **581**
M4   Guards bugler (C) **581**
M5   Guards side drummer (D) **581**
M6   Bass drummer (D) **581**
M7   Guards euphonium (D) **581**
M8   Guards trombone (D) **581**
M9   Guards standard bearer (tin flag) (C) **581**
M10   Beefeater (D) **581**
M11   Regimental mascot (ram) (C) **581**
M12   Life Guard trooper on foot (D)
M13   Horse Guard trooper on foot (D) **581**
M14   Sentry box (E) **591**
M15   Life Guard mounted (D) **582**
M16   Horse Guard mounted (D)
M17   Household Cavalry mounted standard bearer (C) **582**
M18   Household Cavalry mounted kettle drummer (C) **582**
M19   Household Cavalry mounted bugler (C) **582**
M20   Household Cavalry mounted helicon (bombardon) (C) **582**
M21   Desert patrol (French Foreign Legion) on camel (C) **591**
M22   Khaki British officer with pistol (E) **584**
M23   British paratrooper (E)
M24   British soldier with machine gun (E) **584**
M25   Mule (D)
M26   Provision sacks for M25 (B)
—   Khaki soldier lying firing rifle (E) **584**
—   Khaki soldier kneeling firing rifle (E) **584**
—   Khaki soldier advancing fixed bayonet (E) **584**
—   Khaki man with mortar shell and mortar (D) **584**

—   Stretcher party (C) **584**
—   Mule carrying two stretchers (C) **584**
Guards drum major (E) **581**
Guards band cymbals (E) **581**
Guards band fife (E) **581**
Guardsman present arms (E) **581**
Guardsman standing firing (E) **581**
Guardsman kneeling firing (E) **581**
Guardsman lying firing (E) **581**
Highland officer (D) **581**
Highland piper (D) **581**
Highlander, foreign service helmet, lying firing (D) **581**
Highlander standing firing (D) **581**
Highlander kneeling firing (D) **581**
(The flock spray process was used on guardsmen's and Highlanders' head gear, a method also used on farm and zoo animals.)
HM The Queen mounted, trooping the colour (C) **582**
Mounted Royal Scots Grey kettle drummer (C) **583**
Guardsman at ease (E) **581**
Mounted Royal Scots Grey trombone (C) **582**
Mounted Royal Scots Grey bugler (C) **582**
Mounted Royal Scots Grey tuba (C) **582**
Mounted Royal Scots Grey fife (C) **582**
Mounted lancer (C) **582**
Mounted lancer officer (C) **582**
Mounted guards officer (D) **582**
Mounted hussar (C)
Mounted hussar officer (C)

Cowboys and Indians
1   Indian chief with ritual object (D) **585**
2   Squaw carrying papoose (C) **585**
3   Indian with rifle (E) **585**
4   Indian stalking (E) **585**
5   Indian with pipe (E) **585**
6   Indian in canoe (E) **585**
7   Totem pole (D) **585**
8   Fire and cooking pot (D) **585, 586**
9   Indian on horseback charging (D) **585**
10   Indian on horseback with rifle (C)
11   Cowboy kneeling firing (E) **586**
12   Cowboy standing firing (E) **586**
13   Cowboy on horseback firing (E) **585**
14   Cowboy on horseback with lasso (C)
     Cowboy on bucking bronco (C) **586**
     Cowboy on rearing horse (C) **586**
     7th Cavalry officer (B) **586**
     Horse (with base on head) kicking back (B) **586**
     Cowboy with knife (E) **586**
     Cowboy with lasso (E) **586**
     Cowboy gunslinger (E) **586**
     Cowboy tied to tree (C) **586**
     Cowboy playing guitar (D) **586**
     Cacti (D) **586**
     Royal Canadian Mounted Police on foot (D) **586**
     Royal Canadian Mounted Police on horseback (C) **586**
     Indian chief crawling (E) **585**
     Brave with tomahawk and shield (E) **585**
     Brave seated with tom-tom (D) **585**
     Chief kneeling firing rifle (E) **585**

Indian girl carrying pot on head (C) **585**
Indian brave with spear (E)
Indian brave crawling (E)
Cowboy with US mailbag (D) **586**
Sheriff (D) **586**
Bandit with two pistols (D) **586**
(The last three figures listed are direct copies in aluminium of Timpo cowboys.)

Knights
Mounted crusader (C) **588**
Mounted knight (C) **588**
Knight with sword raised (C) **588**
Knight with Morning Star (C) **588**

Salvation Army/Circus/Military Band
Bass drummer marching (C) **593**
Side drummer marching (C) **593**
Standard bearer with tin flag (C) **593**
Cornet player marching (C) **593**
Saxophone player (C) **593**
Cornet player standing (C) **593**
Side drummer standing with drum on stand (B) **593**
Conductor or preacher (C) **593**
Bass drummer standing (B) **593**
Small tuba player marching (C) **593**
Large tuba player marching (C) **593**
Bandmaster with baton (C) **593**
Trombone player marching (C) **593**

Nativity
N1   Virgin Mary (C) **589**
N2   Baby in crèche (C) **589**
N3   Joseph (C) **589**
N4   King kneeling (C) **589**
N5   King black standing (C) **589**
N6   King white standing (C) **589**
N7   Camel man (C) **589**
FD7   Cow (C) **580**
FD9   Ass (C) **589**
FD32   Sheep (C) **580**
W3   Camel (C) **589, 592**
      Shepherd standing praying (C) **589**
      Shepherd kneeling with head dress (C) **589**
      Shepherd standing, arms folded (C) **589**
      Shepherd kneeling praying (C) **590**
      Black King with gift (B) **590**

Circus
C1   Girl circus rider on horseback (B) **587**
C2   Clown in baggy suit (C) **587**
C3   Clown with umbrella (C) **587**
C4   Lion tamer with whip (C) **587**
C5   Lion clawing (D) **587**
C6   Tiger climbing onto tub (also issued as lioness) (C) **587**
C7   Ringmaster (issued in red and black jacket) (D) **587**
C8   Seal with ball (C) **587**
C9   Showman (C) **587**
C10   Circus ring (B)
      Seated lioness on tub (C) **587**
      Tub for performing animals (D) **587**